CAREER EXCELLENCE

Volume - I

G. Ram Kumar

ATLANTIC
PUBLISHERS & DISTRIBUTORS (P) LTD

Published by

ATLANTIC

PUBLISHERS & DISTRIBUTORS (P) LTD

7/22, Ansari Road, Darya Ganj,
New Delhi-110002
Phones : +91-11-40775252, 23273880, 23275880, 23280451
Fax : +91-11-23285873
Web : www.atlanticbooks.com
E-mail : orders@atlanticbooks.com

Branch Office
5, Nallathambi Street, Wallajah Road,
Chennai-600002
Phones : +91-44-64611085, 32413319
E-mail : chennai@atlanticbooks.com

Printed in India at Nice Printing Press, A-33/3A, Site-IV, Industrial Area, Sahibabad, Ghaziabad, U.P.

DEDICATED TO

My brothers and sisters across the globe who aspire to achieve excellence in their careers

A PRAYER

O God!

Grant me...

...the SERENITY to accept the things I cannot change,

...the COURAGE to change the things I can,

...and the WISDOM to know the difference.

– Dr. Reinhold Niebuhr

AUTHOR'S NOTE

Let's face it. Today's world is brutally competitive. To get ahead you need to have necessary skills as fire-power. It is a dog eats dog world. The writing is clear on the wall: Only the best of the breed will get noticed and surge ahead; others will be left behind in this grand race towards excellence. *Career Excellence* is but one small attempt in equipping you to take on the various challenges that confront you in your career journey.

Just as the title implies, this book is designed to guide the reader towards the path of career excellence. It covers the entire gamut of an executive's career – right from preparing winning CVs for your first job to staying at the top as effective CEO and beyond. This book will serve as an essential companion to both existing and aspiring managers.

This book provides clear and common-sense guidance on developing the necessary skills in your career journey. Whether you are ahead as a CEO or still hoping for your first management job, this book is for you.

Career Excellence is, I would prefer calling, a collection of essays. It is a logical and pragmatic guide to self-improvement. This book will aid you by providing you, to say the least, power-packed practical tips, and thought-provoking ideas supplemented by relevant instances and illustrations.

This is one book which is devoid of statistical stuff or complex theories. Everything is simple, straight-forward, down-to-earth. There are no management fads. Deliberately, I have kept jargons out of this book. Reading this book, I am sure, will be a rewarding experience. After you finish this book, I am doubly sure that you will benefit greatly if you can contemplate on the ideas and put them into practice in your everyday life at workplace.

My hope is that the book will go a long way in contributing to individual development and be used as either a rapid read by a busy senior executive, a reference book or a basis for discussion and study in business and corporate development programs.

I would be most happy and consider that my labor has not been in vain if this book helps you in realising your full potential, achieving success, not just in your job but in your career as well and puts you on the way to career excellence!

Read on to know more and let me know how you get on.

G. RAM KUMAR

PROLOGUE

As you would have seen in the table of contents, this book covers a wide range of topics that are pertinent and useful for the modern executive in this complex, ever-changing corporate environment. Some are too preliminary, going back to basics, yet I couldn't help without them. Just in case you need it, I thought it would be useful.

Writing this book has been an enriching and exhilarating experience altogether. I had the opportunity to observe and learn a lot more things.

Hope your reading experience will be as rewarding as I had writing this book.

It was the American poet Robert Frost, who quipped :

> "The brain is a wonderful organ; it starts working the moment you get up in the morning and does not stop until you get to the office."

I hope we can change this situation. Many of us are conditioned to accept less than what we can be. We will have to join together in changing this mindset.

Some topics might seem to be repeated but without them the text would not be complete. Yet I have ensured that they don't overlap much.

As time changes so does almost everything. Much of what seems to be relevant today will become out of sync tomorrow. Relevance today guarantees irrelevance in the long run. However, there are certain skills that stand in good stead throughout your career. Life-making skills like how to build a better personality, communicate effectively, sport the right attitudes, think positive, believe in yourself, value dignity of labor and people, thrive in change, take on trials and tribulations of your career, manage time, people, conflicts or stress, quality consciousness in your pursuit of excellence, provide top quality leadership and human values just go beyond being merely relevant skills. These are enduring skills that will not change for a long time. Mind you, the stakes are a lifetime!

As with any endeavor, everything starts with the self. Why, even your act of picking up this book is an instance of self-effort to know something and gain knowledge. To benefit fully, you must have the interest, opportunity and time to read this book and practice the ideas put forth. This book is replete with quotations just to reinforce the points.

If you are looking for instant quick-fixes or a bag of tricks this book is not for you. Let me make it clear that there is nothing new I have got to say, only I present things in a new perspective.

Though none can spoon-feed yet this book will, at best, serve as a road map for you in your long career journey aiming at achieving career excellence.

"Strive for perfection but settle for excellence" is the basic theme of this book. About 100 topics are presented and you will have enough opportunities to look at things from a new angle of vision. All topics are easy-to-understand and easy-to-apply and grounded in practicality.

Remember, we are spending about 50% and at times more than that of our wakeful hours everyday for almost half of our lives at work. It is a long and exciting journey. To make that journey less tedious and free from roadblocks and potholes we need to learn and practice some tips. Times have indeed changed. Today, it is no longer enough to be the best. It is crucial to be the best among the best, to excel and to be at the top in everything we do. This book will just help in achieving that.

I wish you well on your journey.

CONTENTS

Author's Note	*vii*
Prologue	*ix*
The Making of Career Excellence	*xiii*
1. The Quest for Career	**1–56**
The Value of Work	3
Identify the Right Job	4
Six Ways to Get a Job	8
Winning CVs	13
Interview Skills	31
FAQs in Interviews	41
2. Career Launch	**57–69**
Your First Job	59
Adapt with the Environment	64
3. Communication Skills	**70–127**
Get it Right with the Basics — Reading, Writing, Speaking	75
The Art of Public Speaking	89
Presentation Skills	115
Technology Aids Communication	122
The Seven Cs of Effective Communication	126
4. Business Etiquette and Personal Grooming	**128–163**
Seven Ways to be the Perfect Gentleman	130
(1) Sport the Professional Look	131

	(2) Addressing People	135
	(3) Managing Emotions	138
	(4) Table Manners	143
	(5) How to be an Official Diplomat?	146
	(6) Treating Visitors	149
	(7) The Art of Conversation	150
	Technology Etiquette	157
5.	**Personality Development**	**164–201**
	Seven Qualities of Successful People	164
	(1) Goal Setting — Think Big, Dream Big, Achieve Big	167
	(2) See Beyond the Horizon	171
	(3) Positive Thinking — Positive Living	172
	(4) Failure is Never Final	175
	(5) The Winning Edge	182
	(6) Attitude is Everything	187
	(7) Belief in Oneself	191
	Image-building — Your Personal Brand Identity	194
6.	**Time Management**	**202–213**
	Today is My Time	211
	The Value of Time	213
7.	**Be the Ideal Subordinate**	**214–232**
	Nothing Comes Free	220
	Thriving in Change	222
	Four Follies to Avoid	226

THE MAKING OF CAREER EXCELLENCE

I hope this book would reflect the best I have been able to put into writing about what I have learned through reading, observing and by the experiences gained from people who are around me.

Ever since my high school days, I started reading books as a hobby. Soon, my interest grew in books and I became a voracious reader enrolling in local libraries and read whatever books my hands could lay upon. However, I was very choosy about the stuff I read. Obviously, comics & novels didn't hold my interest for long.

To start with, I read with interest the lives of great people — autobiographies & biographies. Then I developed a keen interest for self-improvement books. At the same time, I developed a healthy practice of jotting down key points in a notebook so that whatever I read didn't go with the wind!

I began collecting quotations, anecdotes & interesting write-ups and these were of much use in writing *Career Excellence.*

When I started writing essays on a few topics I never imagined that I would end up with a two-volume book on executive career development. With the progress of each essay, new ideas emerged and this set me thinking about a book on career excellence. Then the more I thought about it, a fixed idea about the content, layout of the book took shape in my mind and I earnestly set about writing this book.

As the book progressed, many new ideas & thoughts came up, coupled with my own experience in the corporate world and I have made the best use of the same in this book.

No book is ever the product of one person's efforts, and certainly this one was no exception to that. I am grateful to many people for help, both direct and indirect, in writing this book.

At the outset, I am greatly indebted to my teachers, past & present — even now, long after I finished my formal education I consider myself a student of people — for providing me with the rudiments of learning and it's been a passion for me to learn & discover new things on a continuing basis. Every day is a voyage of discovery for me. I regard every meeting with new people as an opportunity to observe, learn & practice the best things they offer.

I am thankful to my mother Mrs. G. Usha who is a source of spiritual enlightenment for me. But for her, I would not have imbibed the meticulousness in everything I do.

I am enriched by the varied discussions I had with my father Mr. S. Ganapathi on management practices, various facets of people — their culture, motives and much of what I have told in this book comes from the rich experience he gained in his long and exciting innings with corporate giants. We often have a great deal of time discussing ideas and analyzing business practices that are in vogue.

Most importantly, I would like to convey my heartfelt thanks to my uncle, Mr. K. Balasubramanian who founded SKetch — an NGO for women empowerment, for being a great source of encouragement in writing this book. Being an intellectual himself, he actively encouraged me to write this book and provided valuable advice. I am sure anyone interacting with him will be amazed at his intellectual abilities, fresh ideas that are thought provoking. If it weren't for his continued support and encouragement this book wouldn't have seen the light of this day.

I owe a great deal to my sister Ms. G. Lakshmi Priya who, despite her busy schedule, helped me in proof-reading the manuscripts with great attention to detail and care.

Special thanks are due to my publisher Atlantic Publishers and Distributors for bringing out this book in two volumes in record time. I am immensely grateful to Dr. K.R. Gupta, Chairman who offered me much help at every step of the publication process. Also, the editorial team was very helpful in editing the book.

This is my first offering as a writer and I very well know that without doubt, a book of this magnitude may have errors, omissions and over-simplifications, for which I take absolute responsibility, while hoping that the rest of the material will be enough to bring new insights and help readers to find the path to career excellence.

G. RAM KUMAR

1

THE QUEST FOR CAREER

The Genesis for a life-long pursuit

- The Value of Work
- Identify the Right Job
- Six Ways to Get a Job
- Winning CVs
- Interview Skills
- FAQs in Interviews

Work keeps us from three evils
Boredom, vice and need

—Voltaire

Let's start with a basic question first. Why do we want a career? The answer is simple. In most cases a career is necessary to make a living. Agree it or not, for most of us, work is synonymous with financial and social security. Our lives revolve around our careers. Without our careers we would be nowhere.

Every job holder all over the world basically aspires for a job that enables them to earn a livelihood. Not much difference between daily wage laborers and us. The only difference is they are blue-collared and we are white-collared.

Our careers are crucial and important for us. One universal fact is that our life, to a large extent, is molded by our careers — the profession we take up, the company we work for and most importantly the compensation we get paid for our services.

A job career assumes significance in the light of the following factors:

1. Basically it is a means to make a living.
2. It gives us a specific identity by making us somebody out of nobody.
3. Power and social status stem out of our job careers.
4. It gives us a means to spend and channelise our energies on a life-long pursuit of a vocation. (Whether we enjoy our career or not is altogether different matter!)
5. It shapes our outlook and attitude towards every thing we come across.

As many vocations so many careers. Today, we have got a bewildering array of careers to choose from. It's all upto us to make our choice. And this choice may be dictated by many factors such as knowledge gained through qualifications, skills developed by experience and talents & temperaments that are inherent in us.

The end of college is the beginning of our careers. We start our careers with high hopes, dreams and visions of success. Soon we face the harsh realities on ground when we find ourselves in the vortex of real-world problems and challenges. When the going gets tough we are baffled as how to cope up with the complexities of the corporate world. Here is where our knowledge, experience, skills and talent should stand in good stead.

But, in most cases, that is not to be. Only now we wake upto the multitude of problems and obstacles that confront us. There are only two options to deal with them. Either find a way to solve or make your way out. There is nothing in between. Those who are geared upto meet the challenges head on will have chances to continue and can look forward to a strong career and for others there is no place to carry on. They will have to drop out mid-way.

Career journey is a long one spanning three to four decades where we spend our best and active phases of our lives. To make that journey exciting, fulfilling and rewarding one we need to pick up lot of ideas enroute, apply best practices, benchmark against the best, cross new milestones with every accomplishment, consistently and in the end of your grand endeavor... win!

Simply put, today's modern business challenges call for people who have the guts to take the bullet in the chest and not run away showing their backs like scared rabbits. Today's corporate world demands the best and the toughest and what prevails is only the ancient law of the jungle: it is the survival of the fittest!

A SPECIAL PLACE

There is a special place in life, that needs my humble skill,
A certain job I'm meant to do, which no one else can fulfill.

The time will be demanding, and the pay is not too good,
And yet I wouldn't change it — even if I could.

There is a special place in life, a goal I must attain,
A dream that I must follow, because I won't be back again.

There is a mark that I must leave, however small it seems to be,
A legacy of love for those who follow after me.

There is a special place in life that only I may share,
A little path that bears my name waiting me somewhere.

There is a hand that I must hold, a word that I must say,
A smile that I must give and tears to blow away.

There's always a tomorrow and the best is yet to be,
And somewhere in this world I know there is a place for me.

—Author Unknown

Our careers are like the game of tennis — those who don't serve well enough end up losing. Your career is a challenge! Go ahead to take on the world!

The Value of Work

God created man to work, work is man's greatest duty.

Man is nothing, he can do nothing.
Achieve nothing, fulfill nothing without working.
Working is man's most dependable function.

If you are poor – work.
If you are rich – work.
If failure discourages you – work.
If success encourages you – work.

If you have been burdened with unfair responsibilities – work.
If you have been entrusted with deserving responsibilities – work.
If you have not been paid fairly – work.
If you have been paid handsomely – work.

When dreams are shattered – work.
When hope seems dead – work.
Work is the greatest stress-buster.
Then work is the mightiest morale-booster.
Work is the best boredom-beater.
Work is equally effective disease-fighter.

If you neglect your work, you invite worry, fear, doubt and debt.
Work is the greatest solution for all the problems.
So work, work, work.
And work sincerely.

—Anonymous

And remember to give your best in whatever work you do!

Identify the Right Job

Find a job you love and you'll never have to work a day in your life.

—Jim Fox

Everyone wants to get a job. But none gives a serious thought to the question "Am I getting the right job?" For the right job gives you immense satisfaction with your choice and reflects in the work you do. You feel at home even at work.

With right qualifications in your kitty you are out looking for a job. Don't take all the job offers that come your way. Pause and proceed. For every job has its own pros and cons. You need to carefully look at the prospects a particular job may hold and take your decision. Let your first decision be the right one so as to avoid regretting sooner or later.

More often, our desperation to get a job lands us in jobs we don't like, we don't fit and jobs which are not in line with our real interests, temperaments and liking. Many people blunder and end up disillusioned in their first jobs. Only if they had cared to check out on a few crucial factors beforehand they wouldn't have hit the wall.

Before blindly accepting the job offer due to the dictates of necessity, however, you must take a hard look at these factors:

1. Suitability of the Job

First things first. Ask yourself whether you are qualified professionally to handle the job. If you are proceed further.

The reason why the right qualification is necessary is due to the fact that many professionals either get exploited by under-employment and burn out fast. The zeal and enthusiasm fizzles out quickly when they find someone with lesser qualifications doing the same job as theirs. They suffer from low morale and start looking for better jobs elsewhere. A shaky start doesn't augur well in the long-run.

In order to avoid such situations it is pertinent that your academic qualifications must commensurate with the job you are about to sign up.

2. Right Place for Top Growth

To find out the right company for top growth in your professional career you must do a lot of fact-finding before you sign on the dotted lines.

The right organisation is one which measures to *your* expectations. It is a place which provides you the right environment. Environment plays a key role in bringing the best out of you. It does as much for our growth as our individual growth. The environment should stimulate you to work hard, encourage creativity and innovation and thereby use your skills and knowledge that is both helpful and beneficial in achieving your professional goals and the organizational goals.

Both personal and organizational objectives are important. The workplace environment is fast changing. Mere brand-image is no more enough to attract and retain talent.

Professional organisations expect and encourage their workforce to grow and develop along with them.

Just a moment! Don't go overboard because of brand image. Advertisements always look great on paper. Offices are plush and look like heaven at first sight. Some times, it is better to work for a smaller company which offers an informal and open work culture rather than big, blue-chip companies with highly centralized and formal work environments. Small organisations give you high visibility levels which biggies don't. Hence, check up the work culture – formal or informal, open or tightly controlled.

3. Fact-finding

Embark on a fact-finding mission prior to your interview about the company. Gather information from the company website, newspapers and magazines, annual reports. Get to know as much as possible from people you come across about the company you are going to apply for. Research on their mission, vision, objectives and financial results. You will learn a lot about the nature and the kind of the organisation you are going to apply for. It helps you form an idea of the company and mentally prepares you when you meet the interviewers. It provides you the necessary stuff to shoot off the right questions at the interview.

4. Interview the Interviewer

At the end of most interview sessions, you will normally be asked the question: "Do you have any questions about the job?" Don't make the blunder of declining them out of humility or meekness. Grab the opportunity and start shooting queries regarding the job profile, job responsibilities, performance expectations, career growth opportunities, etc.

If you know someone in the company ask him all you want to know. Zeroing on the right company is as important as clinching the right job.

5. Decide on the options

One should never consent to creep when one feels an impulse to soar.

—Helen Keller

Before deciding right away, sleep on it for sometime. Weigh all pros and cons. If the pros outweighs and in some measure for the cons then sign up. Boy! Hold on for a moment. Don't go gung-ho with the job offer at the interview table itself. Thank and request politely for some time to think over. The most common blunder we all do is to say 'yes' before we knew what we are doing. We become blind to every other job when a particular aspect of the job is lucrative.

Never betray emotions when the job offer is made straightaway at the end of the interview. Because I know of one instance where the job aspirant was so glad at the offer that he accepted only to find the compensation not matching his expectations. He was too embarrassed to withdraw or negotiate and he ended up getting below the market rates. So avoid taking spur-of-the-moment decisions and falling into traps.

Be practical enough to know the compensation package you are being offered. Probation period, long-term benefits, perks and leave you will be entitled to, etc are the matters you will have to get into the specifics. Compare the present job offer with others which you might have got and then decide.

Look Before You Leap!

Prepare yourself to accept challenges. Choose a career that interests you, but never forget to excel if you want to be acknowledged.

—Kiran Karnik

A few ground rules before accepting an offer will help in taking the right decisions. Never accept thankless jobs. Later, you will be thankful you did not.

Think twice before accepting a job that:

- Entails you to work in a place without windows.
- Wants you to work for people with questionable character.
- Requires you to travel extensively.
- Involves working under deadlines (work pressure).
- Needs people to work late hours on a regular basis.

Get it right with these questions also:

- Location of workplace — Convenience of commuting.
- Job timings — a regular 9 to 5 job or shift system?
- Whether the job requires relocation?
- Whether the job is transferable? If so, how frequent and where?

By knowing the answers for these questions you will be in a better position to evaluate your personal comfort level with the job expectations. You must believe in yourself that you are capable of doing the job. When you are satisfied with your prospective employer ask one last question to yourself: "Will I make the perfect fit into the job and the company?" If you say a resounding 'Yes' then you can go ahead to sign on the dotted lines.

Once you do that there can be no looking back. You have to give your professional best. Simply put, there are no stops for top performance.

Don't believe all you hear. Research independently and decide. It is your career and as such it is your responsibility to take care of yourself. Be smart by choosing the right job that is in line not just with your qualifications and aspirations but also with your temperament, convictions and long-term career growth.

Finally, before you make your first move it's always prudent to,

Think before you act,
Read before you sign.

Get your choice right by identifying the right job. Because when your first job is the right job with the right company, you will have a grand head start for a great career!

Six Ways to Get a Job

The man who wants to do something will find a way;
a man who doesn't will find an excuse.

—Stephen Dolley Jr.

Job search is a well-planned activity which shouldn't be done in a rush or in a slip-shod manner. Following a course of action, pre-determined and organized will yield the expected results. Looking out for the right job commensurate with your qualification, experience, domain expertise and talents & skills can be tough and taxing. At times, when the going gets tough and the economy is recession-hit you will have to leave no stone unturned in your quest for landing in the right job.

To make meaningful headway and increase your chances of getting the real break, explore these six avenues:

1. Placement Agencies

For freshers this is a great avenue to find jobs. Register yourself with reputed placement agencies. Consistently follow up and never miss any interview they may arrange for you. Normally, you will be asked to submit two or more copies of your resume, passport size photographs and modern placement consultants require your resume in soft copy. A registration fee may be charged and the actual consultancy charges may be collected once you get a job.

The following are the leading placement agencies, amongst others in India:

(1) Mafoi Consultants Pvt. Ltd. www.mafoi.com
(2) ABC Consultants Pvt. Ltd. www.abcconsultants.com
(3) TMI Network www.tminetwork.com
(4) Head Hunters
(5) People One Consulting
(6) Step Stone Consultants

2. Online Job Search

Harness the power of the internet by signing up with well-known online job search websites. You will be kept updated periodically through your email ID about the job openings available for you based on the criteria you have mentioned while registering online. While signing up you may be asked to paste your resume. So keep your resume handy in a floppy.

You will have to check your e-mail inbox as frequently as possible and act fast on the information you receive.

The following lists out popular job-related websites:

1. www.jobsahead.com
2. www.naukri.com
3. www.monsterindia.com
4. www.jobsdb.com
5. www.careermosaicindia.com
6. www.careerindia.com
7. www.jobkhoj.com
8. www.jobcurry.com
9. www.hotjobs.com
10. www.jobstreet.com
11. www.prizedjobs.com
12. www.placementindia.com
13. www.promanns.com
14. www.itjobs.com
15. www.alltimejobs.com
16. www.deevesjob.com
17. www.timesjobs.com

3. Get Networked

Let people know that you are on the look-out for a job. Establish contacts with old associates, friends and just about anybody who you believe would be of help. Expand your network and be pro-active. People would assist in their own way to get you through. Though you may not get a job directly yet people may show you the path towards it.

Never underestimate the effectiveness of this approach since many job seekers have landed in the jobs they seek with ease due to their ability to get networked.

4. Keep Tabs on Newspapers

Newspapers — perhaps the most common source for job information must be read regularly. The 'Opportunities' or 'Wanted' column is a must for a job seeker. Never miss your copy and respond immediately.

The early bird catches the worm. Keep stamps of the right denomination, good quality envelopes and of course your resume ready. You must be able to prepare the covering letter without further loss of time from the moment you see the ad. Also ensure that your resume reaches the addressee before the deadline.

Reading any of these newspapers' 'Opportunities' or 'Wanted' columns will be helpful in finding jobs:

1. *The Hindu*
2. *The Indian Express*
3. *The Times of India*
4. *The Economic Times*
5. *The Financial Express*
6. *The Statesman*

7. *The Hindustan Times*
8. *Deccan Chronicle*
9. *Deccan Herald*

Business magazines will be of much help if you are planning a job change midway through your career. Business India, Business Today, Business World, etc are good resources for job hunt. Subscribe them or at least enroll in a good library so that you don't miss your chances.

5. Career Fairs

Attend career fairs whenever possible. Normally, the organizers of such fairs would give enough publicity and all you have to do is to take at least a minimum of a dozen hard copies of your resume, soft copy of the same and passport size photos along with you.

In most cases, you will be asked to leave your resume and given an acknowledgement with an assurance that you will be called for within a week time or so. In some job fairs you may have to go through a preliminary interview aimed to screen prospective candidates and as such take care to dress professionally. Be ready with the right answers as to the choice of your workplace destinations, job timings, salary expectations, etc. Bear in mind that at such times your ability to make quick but correct decisions could make or mar your chances to land in the right job with the right company.

6. Cold Calling Helps

Cold calling or sending your resume unsolicited to a potential employer works, at times. Professional companies store your resume profiling accordingly so as to build a data bank which will be useful for ready reference for their future HR requirements.

If you send soft copy of your resume, it will be added to the company's HR database. But be ready for a long haul and be clear that you cannot expect results overnight!

Five Things to Take Care

While you explore your job prospects in the above six avenues you should ensure that you are ready with the following five aspects before attending an interview:

1. Professional Resumes

Update your resume every year and highlight relevant skills. Make your resume look professional. Prepare resume afresh every time you apply for a job.

2. Covering Letter

Every resume you send must be accompanied by a short covering letter which should be altered exclusively for the job you are applying for.

3. Do Your Homework Well

Research the industry you intend to get in, the company before you attend the interview. Be ready with answers for tricky questions. Apart from testing you for technical expertise the following are some of the typical questions for which you should have the right answers at your fingertips.

- Tell about yourself.
- Why do you want to work for us?
- What is your USP? In what way you are better than others? Why should we hire you?
- How do you see yourself five years from now?
- What are your future plans?
- What is the reason for quitting from your present job?
- Expected salary?

4. Sport a Professional Look

Sport a professional look whenever you go looking for a job. For it creates a favorable impression on others.

5. Be Punctual

Reach on time, every time you attend an interview.

Don't lose heart if you don't succeed initially. Keep trying doggedly and I am sure you will get the job you want. The six job avenues along with these five factors will work wonders and increase your chances, by leaps and bounds. Gear up to market yourself as a potential employee by pulling out all stops in your job hunt and by adopting job search strategies realize your dream of making a real shift in your career graph!

Winning CVs

Your CV is your publicity material. Make it best and let it speak for you

The search for a job starts with a sheet of paper or at the most a couple of papers — your CV. It's no surprise that even seasoned professionals with years of solid experience grope in darkness when it comes to preparing a good CV. It is understandable because they never went about doing up their CVs ever since they got the job. After all we don't go looking for a job every month.

A good curriculum vitae does lots of spadework. None can downplay the importance and the key role played by a CV in arranging your tryst with the interviewer. Among other things, it makes the interviewer to have a favorable impression of you by projecting you in a positive manner. Before the interviewer meets you, it is your CV that is going to speak for you — introducing you and extolling your qualifications, experience and other details. So make sure your spokesman behaves well while presenting you and sends out the right message and ensures you get a red carpet welcome from the HR manager. Simply, a good CV should clinch you an invite for the most sought-after interview.

Before we begin, let's get it right with the ground rules:

- Update your CV every couple of months.
- Prepare a fresh CV every time you apply for a job.
- Never forget to carry an extra hard copy of your CV when you go for the interview. Take a soft copy too.
- Highlight your best and never expose the chinks in your armor in your CV.
- Your CV must be clear, concise and business-like. It should look professional.
- Your CV must be prepared by you, not by others.
- Never copy blindly from other CVs. For copy cats are bound to get caught and moreover the CV looks phony and doesn't match you.
- Contents matter most. Never tell things which you are apparently not. You can't bluff your way through

a CV. You need to back up with proof to whatever you claim to be. So stick to facts.

Two Types of CVs

At the outset, choose for yourself what type or style of CV is best for you. Though it matters a lot as to what you are actually yet it takes your case farther when you know how to say it.

One type of CV is for rolling stone professionals who keep rolling on without staying anywhere in their career journey. If you had breaks in your job stints, then a functional CV is best for you. In this type, you describe your skills and the list the designations and positions you held lower down. Give a clear, unequivocal overview of what you are good at and how former employers valued your services. Never commit the blunder by telling what you are not good at.

For those with steady career journeys without any career breaks, a chronological CV suits well. List out the jobs and the designation you held in reverse chronological order. To be more clear, start with your present employment. Though this is more traditional and conventional yet it is effective.

In a chronological CV, you will have to mention your experience, education and the relevant skills telling the reader what it is that you have achieved thus far.

Components of a CV

Name

Your name — undoubtedly the most important component of you and your CV must be neatly typed in such a manner that it stands out distinctly when the reader takes the first look. Put it in bold letters in bigger font and preferably capitalize. Avoid appending your qualifications to your name.

Objective

Though it is not compulsory yet good CVs for certain jobs will always speak of the objective of the job aspirant. Here he spells out his philosophy, his capabilities, how he hopes to contribute meaningfully with his qualifications, experience, skills and talent for the organisation. But mind you, all this must be presented in a very crisp and brief manner so as to not exceed a maximum of 3 or at most 4 lines. Lengthy mission statements will not be appreciated by HR managers. So keep it short but effective.

Contact Address and Phone

Do mention your contact address clearly mentioning ZIP or PIN code. Include your phone number prefixing the State code.

E-mail

E-mail has become so ubiquitous in this Age of Internet that a prospective job seeker must incorporate his e-mail ID in his CV for faster responses from companies. Choose a name for your email address which looks and sounds professional. Avoid giving out your Ids that have pet/nick names. Sport a name for your email ID that identifies you clearly or comes close to it. Also, your Email Service Provider must be well known and easy to spell. You may have half-a-dozen email Ids but mention only one email ID which you check frequently.

Education

List them down in reverse order of chronology. There is no hard and fast rule about highlighting your division or class of your academic degrees and achievements. If you managed to merely scrap through, then mentioning about them will not paint you in the right picture. On the other hand, if you bagged a gold medal or a merit scholarship then you are free to proudly mention them. Clearly state the Education Board, College and University along with the Town/ City where it is located and the year in which you passed.

Again, your educational achievements can be classified into academic and technical.

Work Experience

Here too, list out your job experience in the reverse order of chronology. If you aren't formally employed before, you can think of mentioning any relevant experience you gained through social service activities done at your school or college.

Tell about your job designations you had in the organisations you served.

Clearly quantify the number of years you have clocked with each organisation you worked for. Put it in numerals for numbers speak louder than words. Better still, if you mention the month along with the year as experience. List out the names of the organisations in full and the places you worked.

Other Skills

The objective of mentioning this sub-heading is to let the HR people know what value-added skills you are having, over and above, your formal educational qualifications.

Language skills, communications skills, typing skills, computer skills are looked for by every HR executive and as such they are worth highlighting in your CV.

Accolades and Awards

Do mention about any awards or accolades you have received in appreciation of your services and achievements. They make a very favorable impression on the HR executive and project you as a person of substance and achievement. No wonder, while evaluating your CV these details will prompt him to call you for the interview.

Personal Details

Here you will have to talk about your family background and your date of birth & age, languages known, interests and hobbies and finally before signing off, references.

Under family background you can mention your father's name and occupation. Many job seekers fail to do this. Remember that HR managers look out for people with good antecedents. So do mention about it.

Interests and Hobbies

Do not wax eloquent in your CV with details of your interest in gardening, carpentry and the like. This part is just to let the interviewer know what your interests and hobbies are so that he can figure out what kind of person you are. Extra-curricular activities can also be mentioned. Keep it brief by not exceeding a line or, at best, two.

References

No sensible HR manager would dare to hire people without proper references.

A good CV will always have at least two references of people holding responsible positions. Towards the close of your CV, put a side heading titled 'References' and mention the person's name, designation, department and address along with his phone number and email ID. Check out and confirm with the persons prior to putting their names in your CV. They should vouch for your integrity and standing whenever asked for. Choose people who know you well and not the other way round — you know them well.

Keep in mind that as far as modern companies are concerned, a CV without references is as bad as one without contact address.

Finishing Touch

Towards the right hand side corner of your CV's last page type your name without enclosing it in brackets. Leave some space above your name so as to provide space for you to put the signature.

In the same line where you type the name, on the left side, after the margin, put the date and a line below the station (place).

Format for Finesse

A good CV needs to be presented in such a way that it becomes an instant eye-catcher with the HR Manager. Invest your time in formatting and present it as neat and attractive as possible.

None likes to put up with lengthy paragraph descriptions. Put down in points. Bulleting and numbering are a good way to present your qualifications and experience. At the same time don't use fancy bullets like pointing fingers, graphic arrows, etc.

Headings can be made bold to highlight better. Underline important points to highlight.

You must have seen that both the word processing packages, MS Word and Lotus SmartSuite, have model CV templates. Before blindly doing your 'cut and paste' job, pbear in mind that scores of other applicants will use them. So be careful before copying. Seeing the same format and layout in hundreds of CVs will surely cause boredom for the HR Manager. Avoid stereotyping. Refer the templates for getting an idea and set about preparing your own style by consulting people. A cursory glance attracting CV will script your doom instead of the grabbing the attention it deserves.

Fonts

During data transmission through email, different fonts can get distorted. Even a transfer among different computers cannot ensure your fonts stay and look the same. This is due to, among other factors, the difference in the versions of the same software. You may use MS-Office XP but the recipient computer may have only MS-Office 2000 or who knows even, MS-Office 97.

The font must be plain and easy to read. The size of the font should not exceed 12 points except for headings.

The best fonts are Arial and Times New Roman. Desist from using fonts like Monotype Corsiva, Lucida Handwriting, Comic Sans and other fancy fonts. They don't lend a professional look.

Functional not Frivolous

The watch words for a powerful CV would be its simplicity, comprehension, pleasing to the eyes and use of key words.

Fancy fonts, colorful graphics and border decorations are eyesores and are not really going to make your CV attractive. Moreover, they are not acceptable in business world. Just make it simple, concise and look professional. No frills and frivolous art works. Don't lavish your CV with bold, italic and other designs.

Just remember that your CV is not the right place for displaying your creative skills. Keep your CV functional but not frivolous.

Use Eye-catching Words

To save the time of the HR executive, use attention grabbing key words in your CV. Use active voice instead of passive one. Employ the right words that are in vogue in business circles but avoid jargon. Keywords like "CCNA", "8 years", "CIMA", "Trained by", "Exclusively responsible for", "Handled independently", etc are bound to get noticed.

Say it With Numbers

There is a magic with numbers. So, quote statistics if you must. Surely, it attracts attention and numbers mean and say much. 98% in Physics speaks a lot more than the same in words.

The Output

Your CV must certainly be printed in a laser printer or ink-jet printer. Never get it done through a dot-matrix printer. The printout must be in black and white and avoid getting it in color. The days of writing CVs by hand and typing out are gone, forever. So never commit such blunders.

The Paper

A good CV must be readable and certainly interesting so as to stand out from a crowd of CVs. To do this, among other factors the texture and quality of paper helps to some extent. Never go for ordinary or sub-standard papers. Use royal executive bond or executive bond papers. The size of the paper also matters. A4 size is the standard one and acceptable everywhere.

Make your CV scannable

Modern and progressive companies prefer to electronically copy and store your CV in a database so as to refer them in future. A scanner is an electronic device which scans your CV. Software is used to search and present to the HR Dept with the profiles of prospective employees. Typically, the software searches the database where the CVs are stored matching keywords present in CVs.

To make your CV scannable and distinctly stands out when searched adopt the following:

- Avoid stapling your CV. Instead use a sliding pin so that it doesn't leave any lasting marks so as to avoid transmitting distorted image of your CV when scanned.
- Use large-sized envelope since impressions caused

by folding to fit into a small envelope can remove entire sentences from your CV.

- Keeping your CV functional and not frivolous pays rich dividends when it is scanned. Just as told before, fancy fonts and artistic decorations get easily distorted during scanning and at times change the entire look and feel of your CV.
- Keywords grab attention. Higher the number of keywords found, the larger the chances are for your CV to be selected. "M.Sc (Microbiology)", "3 years", "MCSE", "CPA", etc are keywords.
- Leave enough space for margins. Check your CV by clicking Print Preview which shows how it appears when printed.

Scannable CVs, or CVs that are scanner-ready, have an edge over other ordinary CVs. The chief merit with a scanned CV is that the candidate's profile stays with the company for a longer time, thereby increasing your chances of getting short-listed for future interviews. So make your CV scanner-ready.

The Size of the CV

Size does matter. First, understand that the average time for reading a CV is about a minute and a half. So highlight your skills in a clear and concise manner. None likes to read a lengthy and winding CV. Do you?

At the same time, don't trade off brevity for clarity. State all you want but make sure they are all relevant and will help you in projecting you in the right picture.

'Keep it short' is the refrain from most HR managers. If you are a fresher looking for your first break it is ideal and pragmatic to keep your CV down to a single page. But if you are a seasoned professional with 10+ years of experience then confine it to two pages and not more unless it is absolutely necessary.

Escort your CV

A CV should be accompanied by a covering letter. It must express your intent for the position you apply for and briefly explain your suitability. It must end on a positive note. A covering letter must be neatly typed and presented in a standard A4 size paper and ensure that it doesn't exceed one sheet of paper. Sign personally and don't forget to put the date and the details of the enclosures.

Never use your official letter head of the present employer to write covering letters. Customise the covering letter every time you apply for a job. Make it professional looking.

Finally, the texture, size and color of your CV's paper must be the same as that of your covering letter. Also see that you match, as much as possible, the envelope which holds the CV and covering letter. Attach a passport size photograph, if specified. Send always the latest photograph. Get yourself professionally photographed every 2 years or so. Don't let it look like the ones picked out from the rogues gallery. Get the addressee's name and designation right and don't forget to affix the correct postage. Ensure your CV reaches in time.

Verify the Facts

Before you printout your CV, "Check-Recheck-Double check". Verify thoroughly as to the facts and figures. Get it right with marks percentage, dates, divisions, contact address, email id, references, etc. Ensure you send the right message with an error-free CV. Don't make corrections with hand. Do sign the CV at the end and check up the date and place.

Have a zero-tolerance attitude towards mistakes be it typographical or factual. Mistakes and over-writings in your CV portray you in poor light.

Time and again, I have been insisting on neatness for having that professional look. Keep your resume free from ink spills, food stains or finger prints and also from folding it haphazardly. It's the neatness that counts, at first glance, above anything else.

Let your CV be different and stand out from the rest distinctly. It must establish a rapport with the reader. What a smile does to the viewer is what a CV is going to do with the HR manager. Good CVs must warrant the second look. Today's HR managers are smart enough to size up people by merely looking at their CVs. As such, a good CV with its look and feel must compel rather than merely prompt him to call you for the interview.

So get set to present yourself in the best picture with a winning CV. It must aim to make a positive statement and reflect your personality, image and caliber. A winning CV highlights your USP effectively. For such a CV is sure to get the attention it truly deserves and set you in motion towards your goal — getting the job with the invite to the interview being the starting point.

Doing up your CV is not a simple 'cut and paste' job. Writing a good CV needs investing considerable time and effort and when you look at the rules by which a CV is prepared you will agree that a lot of pragmatism, thoughtfulness and business sense go in the making of a good CV. Little wonder, CV writing over the years has emerged as an art and it is still evolving. And there are people who have made CV writing as a profession and it is so in its own right.

However, a well-written CV has its own limitations. Don't expect a CV, on its own, to fetch you the job itself. All said and done it is for the job seeker's job to excel himself in the interview. Understand that a good CV, at best bet, is merely an entry ticket to the interview room.

Finally, what you say at the interview must be relevant with you had mentioned in your CV. Both your words and writing must go hand in hand. So memorise your CV's contents and never say anything at the interview so as to give an impression that your words are contradictory and you are trying to bluff your way to the job.

Remember, a good CV will merely kick start a job-search process and leaves the rest to the hero of the CV. From the moment the job seeker receives the call for the interview he takes over, with his manners and behavior, interview skills and technical expertise, to meet the logical conclusion of the process — see the light at the end of the tunnel with the obtaining of the appointment order. The process itself may be long drawn one yet the ball is set in motion with one small sheet of paper — and that's in all probabilities, must be a winning CV!

SAMPLE RESUMES

Curriculum Vitae

S.K. Narayan
1-56-194,
Musheerabad, Phone No: 040-2767 6767
Hyderabad-500 020. E-mail: sknaryan@rediffmail.com

Objective: To seek a challenging entry-level position in the BPO industry.

Educational Qualifications:

Academic:

2001 — 2004 Osmania University Hyderabad

- B.Com — First Class from City College, Hyderabad.

1999 — 2001 Board of Intermediate Education Hyderabad

- Intermediate (CEC) — First Class from Best Junior College, Hyderabad.

Technical:

- **eDAST** — eDiploma in Advanced Software Technology from CMC Ltd. — A Joint Venture of Tata Sons Ltd and Govt. of India, comprising the following skill sets:
    - MS-Office 2000, RDBMS Concepts and HTML.
    - Programming in C, C++ and Unix.
    - SQL 8.0, Visual Basic 6.0, Java.
    - E-Commerce, ASP and PERL.
- Typing Lower, Board of Technical Education, Hyderabad

Other Skills:

- Good speed in Typing.
- Good fluency in both written and spoken English.
- Fast in work.

Personal Details:

Father's Name and Occupation	:	S.K. Naresh, Jt. Manager (Materials), Cosmos Polymers Pvt. Ltd.
Date of Birth and Age	:	03-09-1983, 21 years
Languages known	:	English, Telugu and Hindi.

Interests and Hobbies	:	Reading, Cooking, Travelling, Shopping, Computers and playing Cricket
Reference	:	Mr. Suresh Kumar, Sr. Manager (Finance), Universal Technologies Ltd., Hyderabad-500 042. Phone No: 3105487

Place : Hyderabad
Date :

S.K. Narayan

A.K. GUPTA

D 104/9A, Indira Nagar,
Lucknow – 226 016.
Mobile No: 98485 26016.
Email : ashishkgupta@yahoo.com

Objective: Middle-level position in Finance.

Career Summary:

- June 1999 — present working as Regional Accountant, Lucknow Region in Rainbow Agro Tech Pvt. Ltd. — a wholly owned subsidiary of Rainbow Inc. USA., a global leader in hybrid seed business with a turnover of over US $ 2 billion.
- August 1996 — May 1999 served as Accounts Assistant for Trident Farm Products Pvt. Ltd., Bangalore.

Areas of exposure:

Overall responsibility for Sales Accounting, Internal controls, Administration, Legal & Taxation compliance for the Marketing Region.

1. Receivables Management:

- Sale Order Processing & Invoicing.
- Debtors Ageing & follow-up action for realization of money.
- Cash Management and MIS Reports on collections & depositing.
- MIS on Sales/Customer Details.
- Collection Forecasting & Follow up with Sales Team on Collections.

2. Regional Accounting:

- General Ledger Review
- Scrutiny of Customer Ledger
- BRS — Management Cash Management
- Vendor bills passing & payments
- Budget Variance Reports
- Accounting of marketing expenses

3. Internal Controls:

- Ensuring compliance with company travel and commercial policy.
- Review of appointment of Distributors.
- Distributors Credit Limit Control.
- C & FA management & Inventory Control.

4. Taxation:

- Preparation & filing of Sales Tax Returns for all States viz., UP, Bihar, Uttranchal, Jharkhand and West Bengal.
- Coordinating with consultants for sales tax annual returns filing compliance.
- Details for Tax Audit/Income Tax Assessments
- Preparation & Filing of ESI returns

5. Administration:

- Managing overall administration & public Relations of Regional Office.
- Administration of Telephones/Electricity/Courier etc.

Educational Qualifications:

Academic:

- 1994 – 1996 Benaras Hindu University Varanasi
  Master of Commerce – First Class
- 1992 – 1994 Modern College Lucknow
  Bachelor of Commerce – First Class

Additional:

- 1996 — Diploma in Taxation Law — Institute of Indian Tax Laws, New Delhi
- 1998 — Diploma in Labour Welfare — Institute of Labour, Kanpur
- 1995 — Diploma in Computer Applications — Ace Computers, Lucknow

Other Skills:

- Good fluency in both written and spoken English.
- Ability to handle pressures and to meet deadlines.

Personal Details:

Father's name and Occupation	:	Mr. D.K. Gupta General Manager (Retd.) Orient Textiles Ltd. Lucknow.
Date of Birth and Age	:	19-02-1974, 32 years.
Languages known	:	English, Hindi and Bhojpuri.
Interests and Hobbies	:	Cricket, Table Tennis, Carpentry and Reading.
Reference	:	Mr. M.K. Agarwal, Proprietor, Prime Software Solutions, Lucknow-226 025. Phone No: 2547 7474.

Place: Lucknow

Date : **A.K. Gupta**

RAMESH CHANDRA
55, 1st Lane, Sri Nagar, Chennai – 600 012.
Ph No: 044- 5578 2145

Objective: Vice President (Marketing)

Career Summary:

- ABC Pharmaceuticals Ltd., Chennai 1999-present
  General Manager (Sales)
- SMR Formulations Pvt. Ltd., Chennai 1994-1999
  Assistant Manager (Market Development)
- Resurgent Pharma. Ltd., Ahmedabad 1991-1994
  Senior Marketing Officer

Work Experience:

Managerial:

- Managing a sales force of 60, selling antibiotics nation-wide.
- Setting sales goals and ensuring their fulfilment – Achieved 35% increase in annual rise at ABC Pharmaceuticals.
- Doubled sales from 35 lacs to 70 lacs for SMR Formulations Pvt. Ltd.
- Expanded market base from 12% to 30% for "Gyno" top selling antibiotic for SMR Formulations Ltd.
- Designed and implemented online software connecting regional offices with corporate headquarters at ABC Pharmaceuticals Ltd.
- Recruiting and training sales personnel.

Education:

- New Institute of Management, Mumbai 1990-1991
  PGDBA (Marketing)
- Phoenix College of Pharmacy 1988-1990
  Bachelor of Pharmacy

Others:

- Participated as key note speaker in 'Sales is Growth' global marketing summit for pharmaceutical industry at Geneva, 2001.

- Presented paper on 'Marketing — New Trends and Challenges' at the National Sales Convention, New Delhi, 2000.

Awards and Recognitions:

- Best Salesman Award — 1992 at Resurgent Pharma. Ltd.
- Top Sales Achiever Award at SMR Formulations Pvt. Ltd.
- Life time Member of Marketing Leaders Club, Chennai.
- Executive committee member, Federation of Pharmaceutical Manufacturers, New Delhi.

Personal:

Father's name and Occupation	:	Mr. Dinesh Chandra, Jt. Director (Retd.) Grow Well Agro Farms Pvt. Ltd., Madurai.
Date of Birth and Age	:	15–06–1968, 36 years.
Languages known	:	English, Tamil, Hindi and Gujarati
Interests and Hobbies	:	Playing cricket, football, watching movies, attending Expos and playing piano.
References	:	Mr. Sanjay Kumar, Executive Director (Marketing) Global Pharmaceuticals Ltd. Hyderabad-500 056. Ph No: 040 – 2785 1249.

Place : Chennai
Date :

Ramesh Chandra

S. Anand Kumar
23, Landmark Residency,
M G Road,
Bangalore-561 002.

Phone No: 080 – 5581 2645
E-mail: anands1980@sify.com

Objective: To seek a challenging career in software programming.

Career Summary:

- Two years experience as Software Developer with Focus Technologies Ltd., Bangalore from June 2002 – present.
- One year experience as Technical Support with Prime Technocrats, Bangalore from June 2001 – June 2002.

Educational Qualifications:

- 1997 – 2001 Sunrise College of Engineering Bangalore
  Bachelor of Engineering (Computer Science) – Passed with Distinction (89%)

Additional:

- 2001 – Diploma in Software Technology – Hitech Computers, Bangalore

Certification:

- Certified by Microsoft, USA as Microsoft Certified Solutions Developer (MCSD), 2003 with registration no < ME10125 >.

Skill Set:

- Operating Systems : UNIX, Linux, Windows 9x/2000 Advanced Server.
- Languages : C, C++, C#, HTML, Java.
- Web Technologies : HTML, Servlets 2.2, JSP 1.1
- GUI : Microsoft Visual Basic 6.0
- Back End Tools : Oracle 8.0, MS SQL Server, MS-Access.
- Scripting Language : Java Script 1.3, ASP, VB Script

PROJECT PROFILE

Project # 1

Project Title : Web-based Collaborative System.

Client : Jupiter Breweries Ltd, Mangalore

Duration : 6 months.

Environment : Windows 98, JSP 1.1, Servlets 2.2, MS SQL server, JDBC, Tomcat, Dreamweaver & JavaScript

Description : It is an intranet application that allows the user to assign members to the project team, allow the team members to post questions and receive answers through discussion forum, facilitates searching the archives, alerts the chosen members if there are any changes in the data base.

Responsibilities:

- Used JSP pages to design the website and Servlets for business logic methods.
- Designed client side GUI using HTML.
- Designed tables using SQL Server.
- Used Java Mail API to bring out the email functionality.

Project # 2

Project Title : Web designing for SV Foods Pvt. Ltd.

Client : SV Foods Pvt. Ltd., Bangalore.

Duration : 3 months.

Environment : Windows 98, JSP 1.1, JDBC, Oracle, Tomcat, HTML, Dreamweaver & JavaScript

Description : It is a web-based application to facilitate online purchase of products. The purchase can be done both by dealers as well as individual customers. Dealers have to submit their request through customized forms and their data is validated against data maintained as a database. Individual customers have to only provide their address and the products would be delivered to their doorsteps.

Responsibilities:

- Developed JSP pages that bring out the various functionalities including the shopping cart.
- Designing of the Home page for the website.
- Coordinated with the client for inputs and implemented the same.

PERSONAL PROFILE

Name	:	S. Anand Kumar
Date of Birth	:	25-06-1980
Age	:	24 years
Father's name and Occupation	:	Mr. P. Sunil Kumar, Chief Manager (Projects) Frontline Constructions Ltd. Bangalore-561 002.
Reference	:	Mr. M. Rajesh Kumar, Senior Engineer, Octogon Projects Pvt. Ltd., # 205, Millennium Towers, Park view Road, Bangalore-561 058. Ph No: 080 – 5542 6987

Place : Bangalore

Date : **S. Anand Kumar**

Interview Skills

There may be others who applied there and could have done the job better than you. But it is true today, and it will ever be true: the person who gets hired is not necessarily the one who can do that job best; but, the one who knows the most about how to get hired.

—Dick Lathrop, *Who's Hiring Who*

The call for the "Interview" is one call which is most-awaited and we always like to receive. The very call itself – be it through phone, email or snail mail is a victory of sorts and news to rejoice for job seekers. Yet many dread to face the D-Day confidently and they go with 'butterflies-in-the-stomach' feeling. Only a handful of job aspirants are really prepared to take the bull by its horns.

As you know, your performance in the interview is critical to yourself being hired or not. It can make or mar your chances of being selected to the coveted job. Literally, it's a matter of livelihood or joblessness. Or if you are just job-hopping it means a better job with fat pay packets and perks. Either way, you just can't take the call for an interview lightly. You will have to prepare yourself for success in bagging the job which is hard to come by in these days of cut-throat competition from people who are smarter than you. With the mastery of interview skills you can outsmart those big boys and be on track towards the job desk.

When you attend an interview your objective is to impress the interviewers by your manners and technical skills so as to project yourself as the only person who is most suitable for the job. Interviews always give nerves to job seekers. Yet by preparing yourself well for the D-Day you can glide over smoothly and get results.

At the outset, you will have to keep in mind that in an interview the first impressions you make are important and lasting. Qualifications, experience, technical expertise by themselves will not clinch you the job. Remember that in this highly competitive job market, it is no longer enough if you are the right candidate but you will have to be the smart candidate too! You need to market yourself as the best candidate by employing some soft skills that help you in effectively marketing you – interview skills.

The Spadework

Attire and Appearance

- The first and foremost aspect to take care is your external appearance. Your appearance is what initially counts for others. Remember that "First impressions are often lasting ones". You must be impeccably dressed and well-groomed before you attend an interview. Put in your best appearance and dress. Everything from the way you put your tie to your shine in your shoes matter. So don't leave anything to chance to sport a professional look.

- Appear confident and having positive thoughts reflects in your face.
- Be cheerful and let it be infectious.

Accessories

- Keep the accessories you intend to carry to the interview to a minimum.
- Do carry your latest resume with at least three hard copies, soft copy in a good floppy, 2 or more passport size photographs. A neat leather file holder will suffice to carry all these and look professional.
- Don't forget to take a pen. Preferably carry a good ballpoint pen. Back up with another in your resume file.

Homework

- Do your homework well. Research the company for which you are applying. Know about their promoters, product range, market, turnover, financial results and in short the entire company profile. It gives you confidence.
- Hone your communication skills and brush up knowledge about your domain.
- Do a SWOT analysis and check what kind of job is acceptable to you.
- Give finishing touches to the answers you intend to offer.
- Consult your folks and make up your mind about the work timings – whether shift system or a regular 9 to 5 job, the city/town where you would like to work and salary expectations. On the spot quick but correct decisions on these crucial matters will give you the edge over other job seekers.

As you Arrive

- Every personnel of the company whoever it may be right from the security guard to the receptionist must be treated with consideration. Mind your manners. People watch and observe. Progressive companies take the views of their employees too when hiring people.

- Arrive in time, every time. Ideally, you must arrive at least 10 minutes before the interview and utilise this time to familiarize yourself with the surroundings and compose yourself.
- Treat fellow job seekers with consideration. Participating in discussions with them will throw up new facts hitherto unknown to you. Use this opportunity to gain knowledge. Never get into any arguments so as to lose your mental composure and coolness. Play safe and be a diplomat. Also desist getting into emotional turmoil like excitement or disappointment whenever you 'interview' those who had been interviewed. Bear in mind that there are people particularly among fellow job seekers who would, out of envy, may say things to demoralize you. Don't believe whatever they say but profit from their experience.
- At this stage don't try to recollect or brush up your knowledge. Don't try to read anything or try hard to recall something. Drive away fear with positive thoughts.

Posture and Gestures

Watch your posture and gestures. Your body language must be in tandem with what you say. Poor manners create bad impressions effectively marring your chances of you being short-listed. Aim to present a pleasing personality of yourself within the short time given to you during the interview. Take care of the body language. The grace, charm and poise with which you carry yourself throughout the session are as vital as any other factor for selection.

- Enter the room only when asked to. Knock and enter.
- Walk in confidently with a steady gait. Don't swagger and take inside only the accessories which you require most.

- Greet the interviewers first with a smile. It puts them at ease. Smile when you shake hands. It is the first rapport you establish with your interviewer. Have a cheerful disposition and proceed on to wish them with a clear and audible "Good Morning" or "Good Afternoon".
- Sit only when you are offered or invited to do so. Sit straight without leaning on the table. Don't cross your legs and sit modestly.
- Make eye contact with the interviewer. If you don't look him in the eye it means that you are afraid to see him and not confident.
- Keep your hands apart without fiddling anything. Keep off your hands from the table. Don't play with paper weights, pens, etc.
- Don't try to read anything on the interviewer's table.
- Never point your fingers at others.
- If the interviewer puts you in ease don't take undue advantage and the liberty to sport a sprawling posture when you sit. Be highly conscious of your manners and gestures. He may be trying to fathom you by his informal manners asking you to relax.

During the Interview

The actual interview is very crucial since the time available is very limited. Within the short time, you must make the best impression about you on the interviewer. An invite to attend an interview is an once-in-a-lifetime opportunity for you as far as that particular company is concerned and as such you must make most of the allotted time to your advantage.

- The first few moments you present yourself before the interviewer is very crucial. Make a positive statement with your appearance, posture, mannerisms and cheerful countenance. It just takes a few seconds for the interviewer to size up you and in those moments it is imperative that you bring out the best in you. Similarly, you can size up the interviewer by his disposition, behavior and the first few words.

- What you say matters a lot just as how you say it. Be mindful of your utterances. The phrase "To err can be irrevocable blunder" appears more apt here.
- Speak to be heard. Your voice should be audible to the interviewer.
- Don't try to conceal facts as to your age, experience or the companies you worked for or the reason for your unemployment, etc. It will be too easy to notice when you try to cover up.
- Stick to facts. You must stand by what you have said in your resume. Your resume and your utterances must be one and the same. Any deviation would arouse suspicion in the mind of the interviewer as to your credibility.
- Don't boost yourself so high lest the interviewer may think that you are thinking too much of yourself and trying to be over-smart. Self-praise is no recommendation. Be humble when you state your accomplishments in your career or academics.
- Never accuse your former employers. The interviewer will think twice before hiring a person who says uncharitable things about his former employer.
- Listen and ponder the question well. Interviewers are smart enough to find out your listening capacity.
- Tailor your answers according to the question and be upto the point. Don't rave and rant. If you don't have the right answers admit frankly. Never try to give wrong or misleading answers. Remember you just cannot bluff your way!
- Give clear answers without any room for ambiguity. Never do the mistake of answering in mono-syllables. Frame sentences to make your utterances meaningful. Moreover, it reveals how best you are in communicating yourself.
- In your attempt to portray yourself as humility personified, don't do it at the cost of being branded as timid and meek. There is nothing wrong in speaking when you are expected to. Use the opportunity to highlight your achievements in your previous job or

your academic accomplishments but ensure that they are relevant to the job for which you are applying for.

- Put into use your presentation skills when explaining technical concepts. Define, enunciate and pepper your explanation with relevant examples.
- Expect bouncers and tricky questions. Answering these convincingly calls for high IQ level and abundant presence of mind.
- The range and depth of your knowledge and talents must be cleverly displayed within the limited time given to you during the interview.
- Avoid name dropping. Contrary to what many believe, it creates a very bad impression and the first impulse of the interviewer is to set the resume aside and forget the candidate for ever.

Towards the End

- State why you are best suited for the job in clear terms. Highlight your USP well and say how it would add value to the job assigned. Don't plead, whine or beg.
- End the interview on a positive note. Before you leave, reaffirm your interest to work for the company. Don't appear too keen or desperate to get the job and don't let that to reflect in your face.
- In most interviews you will be asked the question: "Do you have any questions about the job or the company?" Answer in the affirmative and shoot questions to really know facts but it also portrays you as a serious candidate genuinely interested in the job and the company. A negative answer is the recipe for you being glossed over by the interviewer.

Request for permission and then fire typical queries like:

- ❑ What are your exact job responsibilities and routine?
- ❑ What are the job performance expectations?
- ❑ Whether the job is on permanent basis or temporary like on contract?

- ❑ Probation/Training period, if any and its duration.
- ❑ Whether you will have to sign any bonds or deposit money?
- ❑ Salary and fringe benefits you are entitled to.
- ❑ Career growth opportunities.
- ❑ Work environment and organizational culture.

- Towards the close of the interview ask a few questions regarding the company viz. growth, expansion plans, and expectations about the employee to show that you are interested in the company.
- Don't forget to shake hands with your smile exuding positive thoughts.

Be conscious of the fact that every aspect of you — be it your external appearance, postures, manners, technical knowledge, soft skills and above all your attitude is noted by interviewers. Every aspect has its own weightage in awarding the marks. So give your maximum and hope for the best.

Avoid making a Desperate Attempt

Once a company executive was out of job for quite some time and he approached his friend who held a top position in a big company and as such regularly conducted interviews. Taking advantage of his position the executive went for the interview and answered most questions to the best of his ability. But the interviewer persisted with one aspect in his career shift — why he didn't try elsewhere since quitting his previous job? What made him to be jobless for so long? Why he didn't think of venturing into his own business given the abundance of talent and skill? And so on.

The exasperated executive drew close to his interviewing friend, looked him at the eye and blurted out, "Don't ask these questions. Just give me the job. I am starving".

After the Interview

The period of time after your interview and hearing again from your interviewer can be taxing and frustrating. When you have performed well in your interview why worry unnecessarily? You don't have to fret and fume during the interlude. Just keep hoping for the best but at the same time, be prepared for the worst.

Quite often there could be a series of interviews before the candidate is selected. Be prepared for a long haul without losing patience.

Follow up

Most job seekers fail to understand the value of follow-up after the interview. Follow ups are not a sign of weakness. Just as salesman making follow ups before clinching the order, prospective job seekers too need to adopt this strategy to get the job.

The importance of a follow-up note is high since:

- It makes you to stand out as a person worth knowing by gently reminding the interviewer about you and underlining your worth as a person.
- It projects you as being serious about getting the job.
- It makes the recipient feel that the candidate is a caring, sensitive individual.
- It indicates that you are a person of substance and having soft skills and observing courtesies which is a sign of a well-groomed person.
- It is a second chance to portray you positively.

Follow-up Stuff

- A handwritten note will suffice since normally, it will not be intercepted by secretaries.
- Reiterate your interest in the job with the company and how pleased you were when you came in contact with the organizational culture.
- Express your pleasure in meeting the recipient and thank the interviewer for giving you the opportunity to attend the interview.
- But avoid giving the impression that you are pressurizing and pestering the interviewer for the job.
- Keep it short and upto the point. A well-written note must not exceed three or four sentences.

Follow-ups should not be done:

- Through email since it may clutter the recipient's inbox and if it happens it may be counter-productive to the objectives with which you shot of the follow-up note.
- In the official letter-heads of your current employer. Mind you, it is unethical too.

Before you send, check the spelling especially of the recipient's name and get it right with the designation. All said and done but remember that a follow up note alone will not get a mediocre candidate the job but certainly there is no harm doing it. A well written follow-up is appreciated and it pays to send them if you are really serious about getting the job.

By your countenance and visage, academic achievements and career accomplishments and finally by your attitude and performance at the interview session you will have to send the message that — you mean business.

Keep waiting with patience. You will find your break if you have performed exceedingly well. If not, you will have get down to a honest soul-search and take stock of things so that you learn from mistakes and gear up better for the next interview. Failures can be gut-wrenching and there is no point in letting disappointments and defeats to cow you down. One interview failure is not the end of the world for you. You will have to take things in your stride and carry on further. But always remember when you lose, you don't lose the lesson. With positive thoughts and right interview skills I am sure you will get the job, sooner or later. In the meanwhile, keep trying relentlessly towards your goals. And vow yourself never to stop attempting with renewed vigor and enthusiasm until you receive the appointment order of your dream job!

Look your best, move with confidence, speak with conviction — and the job you want can be yours! And take off towards a great career!

FAQs in Interviews

It is better to know some of the questions than all the answers.

—James Thurber

Interviews are conversations aimed at finding out the suitability of the candidate for the job. Often interviews are dreaded as interrogation sessions but believe me when I say that if you are well prepared, it could be just as pleasant as having a nice time of conversation with nothing to fear about.

Ground rules

- The phrase "Knowledge is power" is more apt in an interview than anywhere else. Knowledge is the key in getting through smoothly in an interview. Have all the right answers at fingertips. To gain knowledge, keep learning. Read relevant stuff before appearing for the interview.
- Preparation is vital. Brush up your knowledge about your domain and leave no stone unturned in your efforts.
- Pause and ponder before you answer. In case you don't get the question right, request the interviewer to repeat once again. There is nothing wrong in it.
- Little knowledge is dangerous. Don't try to give false or misleading answers. Remember you just cannot bluff your way through an interview session. If you don't know, better admit openly. Your forthrightness will be appreciated. However, consistency in displaying your ignorance is a sure fire way to be shown the door at the earliest!

What Interviewers Look for in You?

Apart from testing the technical knowledge and expertise of the candidates, the questions posed by interviewers generally try to fathom out different facets of your personality, amongst others:

- Antecedents – Family background
- Attitude – Positive outlook
- Aptitude – Suitability to the job
- Ambition level – High or low

- Achievements – Past performance track record and caliber
- Communication skills – Clarity of expression, fluency & command over the language
- Listening skills – Sensible enough to listen
- Managerial abilities – Suitability for managerial roles
- Leadership qualities – Potential for shouldering higher responsibilities
- Special skills and talents – Anything extra that would add value to the organisation
- Reliability – Willingness to shoulder responsibility & accountability
- Flexibility – Willingness to relocate, travel at short notice or work in shifts
- Personal integrity – Honesty and credibility

Three Top Factors that Interviewers Look for

Generally, every interviewer will look for the following three factors before selecting the candidate:

1. Your professional competence – How able you are to do the job?
2. Your attitude – How motivated are to handle the job?
3. Your suitability – How well do you fit with the organizational environment, culture and values?

Mind you, they have your whole history – your resume at hand and the interview session is just to have a look at the candidate face-to-face and draw more information from the candidate himself to know whether the candidate is a right match for their organisation.

The interview provides the organisation and the HR people to have a grand size up of you and if you are smart enough you too can avail the opportunity to learn more about the organisation you are going to possibly, work for.

FAQs about interviews

1. What I must do to impress the interviewer?

1. Punctuality.
2. Personable appearance – Professional attire.

3. Body language – Maintaining eye contact, smiling countenance, firm handshake – poise, composure and all that make up a positive body language.
4. Enthusiasm and optimism.
5. Confident self-assured picture.
6. Clarity in thought and speech.
7. Right answers.

2. What do I say when I don't have answers?

When you don't have answers for questions fired by the interviewer, be bold, frank and honest enough to admit your ignorance rather than trying to mislead the interviewer with your imagination. There is nothing like 'losing your face' if you don't have the answers.

If you are answering every question that the interviewer poses, remember that there is every chance that he would come with a googly for which you don't have answers at all. This is just a psychological victory for the interviewer in outwitting your brilliance in answering all his questions.

A honest "don't know" will be graceful and will be appreciated rather than a blah-blah for an answer.

Always, bear in mind, despite your thorough preparation still you may not have the right answers. Under such situations, it is better to admit your ignorance than to frantically trying to cover up. You are just losing your ego, not your prospective job!

3. How does one handle a question on disagreements during interviews?

As many people, so many opinions. Every one is entitled to have his opinion. Don't try to refute your stand or impose your view on the interviewer. Desist from taking strong stance and appear judgemental of people, situations or former employers. Neither take a defensive or offensive stance. Take the middle path and play safe.

Avoid arguing or counter-arguing, getting angry or losing your composure. Don't give any room for emotional upheavals. Avoid provoking the interviewer at all costs.

Often the interviewer's behavior may be to find out how you react to such extremities. Don't fall into the trap unwittingly. Be tactful in your responses and even if you don't agree to whatever the interviewer is saying, don't let it know.

4. **When do I bring up the matter of salary?**

   The ideal time to raise salary matter is towards the latter part of the interview when you are seriously being considered for the job. Let the interviewer initiate the talk about it and if he doesn't then you can bring up. The homework you have done about the salary range for the job you are applying for should stand in good stead now. That should help in negotiating a better deal for you.

5. **What is the proper way to end the interview?**

   Take the cue from the interviewer himself to figure out that you have reached the end of the interview. Have the courtesy to thank him and shake hands warmly before you leave.

   Utilise the opportunity to express your interest in the job and say how proud and happy you would be to work for the esteemed organisation if selected. End your talk on a positive note. And finally, inquire about the next step you might have to take.

The Questions

The following is a list of typical questions fired by interviewers. The answers provided are ideal ones but you will have to tailor them according to the question posed. Acquaint yourself well with the questions as well as the answers but ensure that you sound spontaneous in your replies rather than scripted.

1. **Tell about yourself**

   The classic opener giving the interviewer time to weigh you up. Keep the answer short and to the point. Start answering with confidence with a prepared and rehearsed *brief* overview of your career, beginning with your relevant education, taking the interviewer through your key job changes.

Keep your narrative interesting. Tell about major achievements and career highlights. Use your resume summary as a base to start with. Don't waste too much time on family background and school life. Say about your hobbies and interests just for the benefit of the interviewer to figure out what kind of activities you are involved in.

Do highlight your academic and professional achievements.

Take no more than about two minutes to answer — don't bore with details. On the other hand, don't keep it too short to let the interviewer think poorly about you. Focus answers relevant to the employer and their concerns.

2. **What is your aim in life?**

   Be specific. Avoid giving vague answers like "To do my best in whatever I do". Say, for instance, "I want to become CEO by the time I am so and so age" and list out what you would do to achieve your life goal.

3. **How do you see yourself in the next 5 years? And how do you expect to get there?**

   Be positive. Don't make a blunder by saying, "I would be the same as I am today".

   Say "I would be in a better position than I am today. I would be the manager (or if you know the company hierarchy, be specific with the designation). List out what you would do to get there (e.g., Hard work, commitment, learning, delivering results).

4. **What are your short-term, medium-term and long-term goals?**

   The goals you tell them should relate to their business growth. HR managers look for what their candidates and their goals offer to enrich their organisations. Apparently, you cannot say, "I would like to become the President of this country." Limit your goals to just the short and medium range. Be realistic about goals.

   Tell how you would attain them through learning, experience and achievement in your professional career.

5. **How would you describe about yourself?**

   List out your personal qualities. A line or two in answer would suffice.

6. **What is your USP? Why should we hire you?**

   Highlight one or two key qualities of your personality that you consider unique and distinct. Explain how your relevant experience, knowledge, skills & talent that you have learnt and developed over the years you bring along apart from your positive outlook and attitude would make you the right candidate to be hired.

7. **Why do you want to work for us?**

   Sell yourself as an invaluable commodity. Tell why the company needs you as an employee Talk about how you can contribute to the overall success of the company, and explain how that fits with your professional goals.

   Never start first about what you want. Explain how you can make a definite contribution to the company's problems and goals. Say how you prefer working for the company (MNC, market leader, brand image, etc.) and the kind of experience and exposure you gain and that makes you proud to work for them.

   Don't say "Because you give me higher salary, I would like to work for you". Or "Because no other company gives me job, so I want to work for you".

8. **What do you know about our company?**

   Your homework about the company should stand in good stead here.

   Give an overview of the company's business, products, turnover, market standing, profit, working culture, history, etc. Don't get into statistics lest it would seem very artificial and sound as if you are telling them from memory.

9. **What you will bring to add value to the job?**

   List out top 5 qualities and skills you have which you consider unique and distinct. Ability to think out of the box, come up with new initiatives and solve problems are some replies you can think of.

10. What is it like to work in a team? What qualities do you have to be a good team player?

Working in a team requires you to possess good interpersonal skills and communication skills. Flexibility — the ability to stretch oneself beyond one's limits and reach out to others, to pitch in your mite and join the chorus to make work lighter, pleasure and success. You must be willing to share, care and be pro-active.

Cooperation and coordination to the highest degree is necessary to play a meaningful part in a team. Substantiate what you say with an experience or two of how you are contributing and valued as a team member in your previous/current organisation. But, at the same time, don't get overboard when you wax eloquent about the virtues of working in a team so much that the interviewer thinks that you cannot work alone. Strike a balance and say that you are comfortable working solo and in a team.

11. What are your expectations from us?

A challenging job, employee-friendly work practices, an opportunity to grow and develop with the organisation.

12. What are/were you earning in your present/previous job?

Be specific and honest because they can cross check from your salary slip.

13. How much do you expect, if we offer you this position? What salary are you looking for?

Know your market value. You cannot, apparently, quote higher salary since it simply is out of question when scores of candidates with the same skill sets are available to hire.

Say, "I understand that a job like the one you're describing may be in the range of Rs. ___ p.a."

Alternatively, you can counter it with "It's hard to discuss salary details without knowing more about the job profile or responsibilities".

14. Will you sign a bond for 2 years? How long would you stay with us?

This question is just to test you whether you are reliable enough to be hired, whether you would quit if you get an offer a couple of thousand bucks higher than what you are drawing. Though jobs for life are a thing of past yet companies look for some stability and permanency in their prospective employee's stay with them.

Say, "I am looking for a long-term opportunity where I can learn and develop.

Project yourself as a vital, enthusiastic employee who is willing to offer his services for the growth of the organisation for many years to come.

Your answer should effectively deflect every HR manager's suspicion that you are only 'looking around' to fill up the time-gap till you get your big break — attributes of a job-hopper.

Since it concerns with your loyalty to the organisation express your interest in having a long-term career with the organisation rather than having just a job.

However, answering in the negative to this question is a sure-fire way to be shown the door.

15. **Are you willing to relocate?**

Straight question. Say yes or no. If yes, say, "Yes, for the right opportunity".

A negative answer will not go down well with the interviewer.

16. **Have you applied for any other company? What other types of jobs or companies are you considering?**

Keep your answer related to this company's field. Don't say that you have applied for every Wanted ad in the newspaper. After all, you don't want to portray yourself as being desperate enough to get a job.

17. **What is the reason for quitting your previous job? Why would you like to switch your job?**

The interviewer's motive for this question is to find out whether you had problems in your previous company.

If you didn't, provide valid reasons such as the company closed, employees were retrenched, it was a contractual/ temporary job, there was no advancement opportunity or you wanted a more challenging job/career progression.

Also, emphasise the fact that you have been looking for a positive opportunity to grow professionally in your career.

If you had problems, be as honest as possible, but look for a positive angle and don't ever badmouth your former employer. Give a positive picture of your former employers. Every HR manager would think twice before hiring someone who badmouths his former employer because the same would be done to his company too should the candidate quit and appear for an interview with another company.

If you were fired, avoid saying that your services were terminated. Try saying that the job "didn't turn out to be what I had expected" or "it was not the job match that I had hoped it would be". Then explain briefly without putting blame on your former boss or company. Highlight that it was a learning and professionally rewarding experience that will help you perform better in your new job.

18. How frequently have you changed jobs? Are you a job-hopper?

If your job change is frequent, prepare an answer based on good rationale for your moves. Don't sound defensive. Let your reply be convincing and reasonable.

Some acceptable reasons:

'The company reorganized. A new manager arrived and brought in their team.'

'The company suffered losses and had a massive lay off.'

'The project was completed and hence my contract was over.'

'The company was sold/The company was taken over.'

'They offered me a move that would have meant no apparent opportunity.'

or...

Reasons to avoid:

'I didn't get along with my boss and colleagues.'

'The management policies were not to my liking.'

'My boss was an idiot.'

'They passed me over for an increase in salary/promotion.'
'There was too much work pressure.'
'There was too much overtime.'
'I had problems with my health.'
'I had personal problems that interfered with my work.'

Common psychology shows that when you discuss about a problem, even if it is not of your own making, the interviewer will hold you partly responsible. Show that your choices were for positive reasons.

19. What's your opinion of the last company you worked for? How was it like working for so-and-so company?

A loaded question. Either stay neutral or better still be positive. Never ever badmouth your former employers. Say how it was a nice opportunity to learn and grow and how rewarding and professionally enriching experience it was to serve under your previous employer.

Never commit the blunder of speaking ill of your former/current employer. No sensible HR manager will hire people who talk ill of former employers.

20. Your accomplishments in your previous job?

Give a brief overview of your achievements. Be aware that whatever you say will be cross checked. So back up your answers with proof — appreciation letters and citations, etc.

21. What do you look for in a job?

A chance to prove yourself by utilising your qualification, experience and skills. An opportunity to serve under the organisation and add value to the job you are performing by excellence. To make yourself a valuable team member, a go-getter, result-oriented and thus contributing the best that's beneficial to the organisation on the whole.

22. What would you do when you are confronted with a problem?

This question is to find out your problem-solving skills. Say that you would approach the problem at hand in various points of view, gather relevant information as much as possible, brainstorm with the concerned people and arrive at a consensus to solve the issue. Don't forget to say how you would ask help from others, particularly professionals to get the problem solved.

23. **How well do you work under pressure?**

Be specific. This question is just to find whether you are used to work under pressure (read deadlines) and whether you had prior experience of slogging hard. The response you give also shows whether you are willing to work late hours or pack up lock, stock and barrel at close of business hours.

Your answer sheds light on areas like your ability to handle stress, organise and prioritize and meet deadlines.

However, you can counter with "How much pressure is involved in this position?" Find out what they exactly mean by the term pressure. If you thrive at high pressure jobs, give them some examples. If possible, give examples of situations when you were under pressure to deliver, and how you met the deadlines.

24. **Are you capable of multi-tasking?**

This question is to find out whether you are capable and accustomed to don different hats and come out with flying colors.

Give instances of your previous experience where the job routine called for multi tasking abilities. Also tell how multi-tasking helped you to pick up new skills and learn more. Provide proof of how you are multi-skilled in your field helps to establish that you are a multi-tasker.

25. **Give your definition of the job you're pursuing. Explain your current role and what you do on a day-to-day basis.**

Define and explain the objective and goals of the job. Provide an overview of the duties and responsibilities as well. Inform the interviewer as to how exactly your role fits into the organisation and then proceed to give details of your day-to-day job routine.

26. **Describe your ideal working environment.**

You will have to be realistic and pragmatic in answering this question. Your answer reveals a lot... of your expectations and aspirations.

Let your answer be a blend of pragmatism and realistic expectations. Also, make it sound more relevant to the organizational environment, standard industry norms and business practices.

27. What can you do for us that someone else cannot do?

Here you will have to pitch in yourself as the best candidate with your USP. While selling yourself, leverage on your past achievements and the kind of experience you had and deftly relate how you could add value to the job you are being interviewed for and be useful overall to the organisation.

Or if you are a fresher, highlight your qualifications, special skills and talents you may have. Of course, your enthusiasm and energy you exhibit, positive attitude, capacity to work hard in a result-oriented manner can also be helpful.

28. Would you choose the same career if you were to start all over again?

Don't let your response to sound apologetic about your career. Even if you aren't happy with your choice of career, don't let it show. Apparently, none would like to hire people who are sorry about the past.

No matter how much you despise the career you are currently pursuing, say that it was out of your own volition that you chose the current line of career. It isn't that you were left with no option that you were constrained to go for it. Express your happiness and satisfaction about your present and the past. The basic line is "Absolutely no regrets — happy about my present — proud of my past" kind of reply.

On the other hand, if you are making a complete switch over to a new field, tell that you would choose a field you're now trying to enter if you had it to do all over again. Explain that since you didn't have the opportunity to do so then, now you are entering it.

29. How long have been searching for a job? Why haven't you been able to get a job as yet? Why have you been

unemployed for so long? Why haven't you found a new position before now?

When you can't hide the fact that you have been job-hunting for a while, project yourself as a person of choices. Say that you were choosy about the right job with right company and not taking all the offers that come in your way. Say how you took your own time or bid your time to get the right break because you were more concerned about extending your services to the best names in the industry. And conclude how the wait is well-worth.

A recession-hit economy and tight job market are good reasons to explain that you had a tough time looking for the job you wanted.

This kind of reply portrays yourself as a person who knows what he wants and is sure to get that and goes to any length to fulfill his aspirations. At the end of your reply, the interviewer should have a positive feeling about you that you have been associated only with winners.

30. Choose your option. An easy project with a great scope for visibility and recognition or a low-profile project that's challenge and tests your mettle and professionally-enriching experience?

On analyzing the scenario I would prefer the latter. Because it offers me opportunity to prove my worth and that can help me in every way. Challenges excite me and I would like to meet them.

31. What you don't like to do?

Beware! This a loaded question with which the interviewer tries to fathom a new facet of your personality.

Play the diplomat instead of reeling off your list of dislikes and hatreds.

You don't have to reveal your contempt for Admin personnel or the hatred and fear of Auditors. Deflect with, 'When there's something disagreeable to be done, I try to get it out of the way first. But, I've no particular dislikes'.

32. What would your current boss list as your strengths and weaknesses?

This is just a twist of the good old "List your strengths and weaknesses" question. Don't get caught unawares in the interview room and blink for answers.

As part of your homework, do a SWOT analysis and prepare a list of strengths and weaknesses. However, tact is knowing what to say and what not to say about your strengths and weaknesses.

Obviously, you cannot tom-tom your qualification as strength or your lack of it as a weakness. Or worse still, don't ever say that you don't have any weaknesses at all. The question aims to find out some qualities of you, in your own words that you consider as strengths and weaknesses.

List out at least three to four qualities as strength and try to relate how they help you in your current job. As for your weakness, say some thing that doesn't directly impact your job performance lest it would cast serious doubts about your abilities.

33. What are your areas of improvement?

Weakness can also be termed as "Areas of improvement". Never ever say you have none. It doesn't cut ice with anyone since none is perfect.

Try saying, "I am not good at reprimanding people since I adopt positive approach rather than directly confronting them head-on".

34. What do you think it takes to be a good manager?

Tell them about the qualities of a good manager and the preferred style of management. Describe how it helps in managing people and getting things done.

35. What about the job, offered to you, you find the most attractive? Least attractive?

On the whole, let the positives outweigh the negatives. List out a few solid aspects of the job as attractive but mention only one, that too a minor at that, to be least attractive.

36. How do you rate yourself in this interview?

Be positive. Don't self-boost. Remember 'self-praise is no recommendation'. Even if you have a feeling that the interview didn't go well, don't let it show. Express yourself confidently.

37. Have you any questions you would like to ask us?

Jump at the chance to interview the interviewer! The following are some questions for you to ask:

- Job routines and responsibilities.
- Company business and operations.
- Is there an induction programme?
- Are there any training programmes to be undergone? Duration?
- Performance appraisal systems.
- Career growth opportunities.
- Is there a brochure or any literature I can take away to learn more about the company?
- What is the next stage after the interview — where do we go from here?

Firing questions portrays you as a serious candidate genuinely interested in the job and the organisation. Your interest and enthusiasm to know more about them will be appreciated.

However, instead of giving a blank look and wondering what to ask, do some pre-interview information gathering about the organisation from various sources — friends, newspapers and business magazines, annual reports and of course the company website. This will help you to ask some intelligent questions with which the interviewer will be pleased rather than annoying him with silly, basic ones.

Before you are offered the job asking for salary details is a strict no-no. This projects you as being more interested in what you can get rather what you can give.

Never ever do the mistake of raising controversial issues that the company may be involved with or ask anything that may be taken as questioning the organisation's credibility. This may force the interviewers to mark you as a potential troublemaker and thus you are self-sabotaging your chances of getting yourself hired!

Each of the reply you give may lead to counter-questions. As the pace of the interview picks up, questions may be fired at the drop of the hat and they come in hordes in different types — simple and straight to tricky and loaded. It takes tact, presence of mind to give appropriate (acceptable is good, convincing is excellent) responses, foresight, political correctness and ability to think on your feet quickly. Expect googlies in good measure.

The answers to these questions throw light on a whole range of your qualities. Let honesty, forthrightness and frankness be your watchwords while answering these questions. Never say anything that contradicts your earlier utterances. If you are wrong, apologise and rectify immediately.

Let your answers sound convincing. Don't let it appear like someone has tutored you to say stock replies and you have just rehearsed it thoroughly.

The answers you give throw light on your level of confidence, communication skills and caliber. These three factors are most sought after qualities that every HR manager looks for in every candidate. If you are able to master these, you will easily get through any interview!

Above all, your responses to these questions portray your caliber and if it matches with their expectations, you are in. In most cases, failure in interviews is due to the mismatch between the requirements/expectations and the candidate failing to measure upto such expectations or unable to offer so as to match with the requirements of the job/organisation. So give the right answers with confidence and optimism and the job you seek will be yours!

2

CAREER LAUNCH

Take off to a great career

- Your First Job
- Adapt with the Environment

One step at a time...
A journey of thousand miles begins with one step.

—Lao Tzu

Career launching is an important event in our lives since it is the point of time where we start our long careers. However, we cannot get to the moon straight away. A few issues are to be understood before we proceed with our careers.

Analyse Yourself

Make an analysis of yourself — your qualifications, skills and talents you possess. Obviously you don't have experience. So your first job experience is going to be very much new and exciting. First you must have the aptitude to learn. Else you get nowhere.

Be honest with your self-analysis with the help of SWOT system. For the uninitiated, SWOT stands for Strengths, Weaknesses, Opportunities and Threats. This helps you in gearing up to the future better. Forewarned is forearmed.

You have an idea of what sort of job suits you and in what you are best. Leverage on your plusses and take conscious efforts to turn the weaknesses into strengths.

Your learning efforts in your first job must aim at plugging the loopholes in your knowledge with practical exposure and experience. Seek out the unknown and master it.

One Step at a Time

I am what I am today because of the choices
I made yesterday.

—Unknown

If you would understand the meaning of this great truth, you will be at peace with yourself and others. Obviously, there is no point in fretting and fuming about your position in the corporate hierarchy.

The times in which we live are fast and swift. Every body wants to be a high flyer from the day one and want to climb up in three steps the career ladder even before they learn how to take the first step. Understand that the position and pay that your first job offers is commensurate with your qualification and your personal qualities. You can't always start at the top. But you can start at the bottom and work your way up. 'One step at a time' policy is good and safe. As you will see and realise, those who zoom up fast are bound to come down crashing faster. First walk, then run.

Ever since you finished college you were job-ready. Since then you have been looking forward to your first job. The entire process took a while to materialise... the resumes you posted via snail mail or email, the eager wait for the call that seemed like an eternity, the hurried dusting up and brush up of your college books one last time, brushing up of everything from your teeth to communication skills, interview skills and what not, the 'butterfly-in-the-stomach' feeling on the D-Day, facing the interviewer, another wait that made your heart throb with the question 'Will I?' or 'Not this time', and you got that life-giving call giving your joining date. After that, smiles all around, an euphoria, many pats in the back, a small party celebrating your break and you are ready. You have gone through enough.

You got your break. Your moment has arrived. Now, take the plunge!

Your First Job

Your first job is an extension of your education

Fresh out of college. Loads of dreams. A whole new world waiting to be explored. And you are just waiting to put all those fat books you have spent the last few years studying into practice. Self-assured and confident yet anxious about the new world ahead. To make all those castles in the air real...with your very first job.

Like every other first experience, the first job is one experience which you wouldn't remember to forget. The experience could make lasting impressions in your mind.

Desirables

In your first job, there are a few things that are helpful. Though they are not mandatory yet they are desirable in view of the long-term benefits they offer.

1. Postpone marriage.
2. Starting up with MNCs helps.
3. Start in line functions.

   Choose between:

   - Accounting vs. Audit.
   - Sales vs. Marketing.
   - Production vs. Planning.
4. Start in the private sector.
5. Work outside your hometown.

The Basics

First, understand that your first job is not a job. It is an extension of your education. The first job is the foundation of your job career.

By foundation of your job career I mean that the experiences you come across leave indelible impressions on your mind that are often lasting ones. It shapes your attitude and outlook towards lot of many things.

The first job is a stepping stone to higher levels in the corporate hierarchy. Don't start looking for new jobs when the going gets tough or when someone offers a few hundred bucks more. Stay on for a minimum period of 5 years. The experience provides you a solid base upon which you can build your career.

Be flexible and go mobile. Don't stick to one city/state and get your career grounded. Be prepared to shift anywhere. Travel widens your horizons.

Seven Steps to a Strong Foundation

1. Right Attitude

There are no menial jobs, only menial attitudes.

—William John Bennett

Have an open mind. Never judge anyone or anything immediately. Wait and watch before jumping into conclusions. Having the right attitude towards work and people is as important as the ability to work. Modern companies require their employees to sport the right attitude that is in full alignment with their goals and objectives. To start with you must be a law-abiding employee giving due respect to people, processes, practices, hierarchy and the organisation.

Again, attitude matters most since it measures your altitude. It can spell how far you can go on the organizational hierarchy. Right attitude is one where the mind looks at things with a positive outlook. You are open to ideas and there are no limiting factors to cloud your views and opinions about people and their ideas.

2. Get Networked

Get to know people and be friendly with them. Your work may warrant, at times, getting in touch with different people. During such occasions their support and guidance will be very much valuable and useful. But irrespective of your work requirements it's always good to know people. Coffee and lunch breaks are times to mingle with people across the organisation.

Come out of the shell. Don't restrict your circle with just among those in your department. Reach out to people from across functions.

3. Learning the Ropes

Your first task is to secure yourself — to transform the slippery toehold you have gained into a firm foothold. For this to happen you must become technically competent.

Technical competence comes when you learn the job thoroughly. Transform the theoretical knowledge gained in your years of study into practical and workable application to the job you do.

Learn as much as possible — across functions. The more you learn the better. Most novices fail by trying to learn the tricks of the trade. Instead, learn the trade itself. Learn across functions and become multi-skilled. That looks great on your resume.

More than learning what's more important is the willingness to learn. Develop this desire to learn and there can be no stops for you. Many novices are shy of learning lest they would be branded ignorant. When you are struck somewhere don't blink; ask help. People will explain how. Don't live with ignorance. Dispel darkness with knowledge. And as the Danish proverb says, "Better to ask twice than to lose your way once".

Be ashamed to say, "I don't know". Learn and you will never have to say that again.

Invest your time, energy and resources in learning without expecting anything in return.

4. Take Initiatives

Folks who never do more than they get paid for,
never get paid for any more than they do.

—Elbert Hubbard

Without initiatives you are nowhere. You will not get noticed and counted. Initiatives prove your worth and serve as portraying you as pro-active, loyal and committed to the organisation you work for. Higher-ups will start taking you seriously.

Initiative means exhibiting originality, doing a thing on your own volition without being told by someone.

What sets two trainees apart is this ability to take initiatives, to pitch in with ideas and suggestions in order to improve and simplify processes & procedures. "That's-not-my-job", "Why-should-I?" attitudes must go away for good in order to take initiatives. And taking initiatives is one way to get out of the pile and stand out distinctly.

Let me explain the value of taking initiatives with an example.

Three brothers, Jim, Mike and Bill were hired by a company on the same pay. Three years later, Jim was being paid $500 a month, Mike was receiving $1000 but Bill was making $1500.

Their father decided to visit the employer and questioned about the disparity of their income. He listened to the confused father and said, "I will let the boys explain themselves".

Jim was summoned to the supervisor's office and was told, "Jim, our company has just brought a large cargo ship loaded with Japanese electronic items. Will you please go over to the harbor and get a cargo inventory?"

A few minutes later, Jim returned to the office. "The cargo was one lakh units of Japanese stereos". Jim reported "I got the information over the phone from the Port Trust delivery office".

When Jim left, Mike, the $1000 a month brother, was called. "Mike", said the boss, "I wish you would go out to the harbor and get an inventory of the cargo ship which was just brought in by our company".

An hour later, Mike was back in the office with a list showing that the ship carried one lakh units of Japanese stereos, 75000 cameras and 100 camcorders. Then Bill, the $1500 a month brother, was given identical instructions. Working hours were over when he finally returned.

"The cargo ship carried one lakh units of Japanese stereos", he began. "It was on sale at $50 a piece, so I took a two-day option on the whole lot. I have wired a manufacturer in Iowa offering the stereos at seventy five dollars a piece. I expect to have the order tomorrow. I also found the 75000 cameras, which I sold over the telephone at a profit of $25 each. There were 100 camcorders of which nearly 40 were damaged during transit. So I sold the rest at a profit of $75 a piece".

When Bill left the office the boss smiled. "You probably noticed" he said, "that Jim doesn't do what he's told, Mike does only what he's told, but Bill does without being told".

The future is full of promise for one who shows initiative.

5. Be Accountable

It is in the first job we always commit blunder and mistakes and we fear to tread confidently. We try to effectively use the loopholes and make good our escape from accountability. But beware! People always are watching but they just don't point out for whatever reasons.

Being accountable to the jobs we undertake is a sure sign of maturity, courage and confidence. The courage we display to own up mistakes and take responsibility for our actions will show us in the right picture.

When things go wrong, standing up and admitting the faults will only help us to see things in the right perspective and provide us an opportunity to learn from such aberrations. Though it is easy to pass the buck and thank our stars for not getting caught we learn very little except cunningness and tricks of the blame game which doesn't augur well for us.

6. Work on Feedback

Feedbacks are a report on your performance. Be open to criticism and correction. Since it's only your very first job people may point out when you go wrong. Learn. Take feedbacks seriously and positively. They help us being focused by pointing out the anomalies and gaps between the expectations and our performance. Don't lose heart if you are not upto the mark. Every professional is at first an amateur. Give yourself a chance and think how best you get bridge this variance. Ask for guidance from your superior and he will be glad to do so.

Working upon the feedback is more important than merely attending the routine feedback sessions. Start by taking efforts on the areas of improvement. Improve constantly until you exceed expectations. And again improvement doesn't end there. You can just feel satisfied that you have met the standards but improving constantly is a never-ending mantra. The proof of the pudding is in the eating! Prove yourself with improved performance. That way you gain confidence of your superior.

7. Say no to Gossip

The bane of new recruits is getting into the vortex of gossiping and politics. Steer clear from these as they pull you down to an abyss. They spoil and cloud your outlook, attitude and approach. Gossiping and lying go hand in hand.

Never talk ill of others particularly when they are not around. Such behavior is in poor taste. Don't harbor extreme views on persons and things. Those who value work and their time will not waste time in gossip.

Brace yourself to get a few shocks in your first job. After all, everything is not tailor-made for you. For instance, you may have visualised your office as a dream office just as you get to see in films and glossy magazines & brochures. Remember, the size of your office is not as important as the size of your pay cheque.

First job experiences are worth remembering forever. Let self-consciousness give way to confidence and move ahead with firm steps. As with everything else, keep your eyes and ears open always. Tread with care since it could either leave indelible scars or make you a star. Do things that you would be proud about and you will cherish the experience forever. Let your foundation be strong and it starts with your first job!

Adapt with the Environment

Managing the work environment is the key to success.

Your first job. Or your first day out in a new office. You are a bundle of nerves and excitement. Unfamiliar faces greet you and it takes an effort to maintain your sense of balance.

Don't get intimidated by the work environment at first sight. It's a common predicament for most new entrants in integrating with the work culture and feel at home.

Fitting in with the work culture is an important aspect of gaining acceptance in an organisation. You will love to report to work daily if you are able to manage the work environment.

Initially when you came you had a totally different view and vision of your workplace and the people you will be working with. With the efflux of time, you got to see things in their true colors and felt everything is not as rosy as you thought before. The first step in preparing yourself to fit into the environment is to accept things as they come.

Don't Kid Yourself!

First understand this is not your college class room where you can sit with your best chums. Or if you have just switched over to this job get over the hangovers. New environments need new adjustments on your part. Prepare yourself to change for good. People suffer from attachments to places and people. They become too much dependant that it begins to affect their working style and productivity. Places and people shouldn't affect a person in giving out his best. External factors shouldn't drive us. We must be internally driven. Display maturity in your behavior and attitude. Working is a serious business. Don't kid yourself!

Approach Towards People

Bear in mind that your adapting with the environment depends to a large extent by the way you deal with people. People skills will stand in good stead at this juncture.

Be careful while dealing with people. For, they are very sensitive. A few ground rules will help in your approach towards people:

- In your zeal to get across don't pluck a raw nerve. Don't over-reach.
- Give people their space. Over time they will come around.
- Don't rub people on the wrong side. You will never get it right from day one.

- Give due respect to everyone you come across.
- Never make anyone feel small by virtue of your qualifications, experience, knowledge, position, previous company brand image, personal life-style and affluence or family lineage.

Cordiality

Your relationships with co-workers must be marked with courtesy and cordiality. Never pick out quarrels with people over differences. Play the diplomat in you and get it resolved in private by discussing with your superior. Disharmony at workplace relationships could be debilitating making your stay at the organisation a hell.

On the contrary, relationships that are based on trust and confidence, friendliness could spur and stimulate you to perform better. It increases your productivity at work.

There is Nothing Personal About It

Most of us forget to leave our personal baggage at the threshold of our office when arriving for work. Employees who suffer from hangovers from personal lives are headed for trouble. Companies don't look for your personal business to hassle them. Business matters are to be attended with full concentration and dedication. That's what companies expect when they hire people.

Always maintain a good distance with everyone you come across however close they may be to you. Don't wash dirty linen in public. For its implications are not apparent but may come back to you in full blast in the most inopportune time. Companies deeply resent loss of productivity by employees who share their worries and concerns with all and sundry. Be professional and business-like in all your dealings. When you enter your office, it is strictly business. There is nothing personal about it.

Keep Your Eyes and Ears Open

Use your observation skills to the hilt. Merging in with the work culture could be a bit taxing initially. Observe around to know the work style and culture — formal, informal or semi-formal. Understand the hierarchy, behavioral patterns and relationships between executives and departments.

Observing intensely at various things happening around you — people, practices, procedures, etc helps you to unravel the corporate maze in which you are stuck in.

Observing keenly and adopting acceptable practices in line with the organisation's values is the key to adapt with the environment fast. It could be as trivial as coming to work on time or not. If the organisation sports a "It's OK" attitude towards employees arriving late by a few minutes then it is fine for you to come late occasionally. What is fine with one organisation may be a cardinal sin in another.

Again, it all depends on your boss and how he vies such lapses, though they may be trivial. Anyway for the safer side, avoid taking liberties imitating others. Until you fit in and become acceptable and endear yourself to everyone you remain still a new comer and as such you cannot afford to take liberties on your own.

Keeping your eyes and ears open at all times and being alive to the happenings around us is essential to survive and thrive in this complex corporate work atmosphere.

Pitch In

Working outside your job profile may not be all that bad as long as it doesn't affect your performance. Pitch in your bit to help others with their work. You get to know people better and learn their work. Also people look at you as a helpful colleague and their perception changes about you for the good. You get a favorable impression.

Voluntarily pitching in is good but offering yourself gracefully when someone asks for assistance is better. That way you endear yourself to co-workers.

Know Your Profile

Get to know your job profile preferably in writing. Study them thoroughly and know your brief. Learn the workflow of your department. Don't stop with that but understand the business of your organisation and be aware of how other departments affect your functioning. Learn about the goals and objectives of your organisation, target of your team and the criteria for rating your performance.

See the big picture and also know where you stand in there. Also it gives you an idea where your team fits into the entire organisation.

Understanding your job gives you a better grasp in donning the mantle better. Spend the first few weeks to get to know the nuances of your assignment. As you learn and understand better, apprehension must give way to confidence.

One sign which indicates that you have adapted well with the work environment is when you are taken seriously by people. They just can't afford to write-off you.

Fitting in with the Culture

Don't sing solo; join the chorus. Team work is in. Substitute 'I' with 'We'. Go with the flow yet maintain your individuality with your identity.

Every organisation will have its own practices and procedures. What is appropriate and acceptable in one may not be in another or rather the other way round too!

So mentally prepare yourself to make a clean break from your past. Get over the hangovers. Start afresh and look at things in your new environment without any personal bias. Give respect and follow established practices and conventions. Desist from questioning them. Apparently, none likes to be challenged by new comers. Don't find fault with things even if they aren't right. Simply, don't confront. People, particularly, old-timers resent.

Proceed with caution. At first, things would look different and you could start questioning the way they are. But as you get familiar, you will gain understanding and be in a position to relate better why things are done in a particular fashion and thus you will be able to appreciate. So give people the time and space and eventually when you fit into the culture you can go about fixing things which aren't right. Avoid sporting a reformist's stance. Setting out to correct things as a new comer will spell disaster and nothing is worse than this to start your career in a new organisation. None can appreciate a new comer picking out faults of well-established conventions and practices. So first settle down and then think what you can do about.

Get to know of the people with whom you are going to work. Go beyond the customary 'hello' to acquaint yourself about them. Make them talk about themselves and you will gain a better idea. Use coffee and lunch breaks to interact and socialize. That way you send out the right signals and message by your words and actions. By doing so, you mean business and you are taken seriously.

Don't let a welcoming handshake turn into an arm-wrestle down the line by your words and actions. Let your handshake strengthen the bond with your colleagues and the organisation and transform into a joyous embrace as you endear yourself. And then you know you have fit into the culture.

Take care of the following three basic criteria which can spell success or doom in your new work environment.

1. Performance — Your work speaks for you. So ensure that you give a top-notch performance.
2. Attitude — Right attitudes serve as building blocks for your career. Project positive attitude always.
3. Behavior — Your behavior must be dignified and professional throughout.

And finally play by the rules and be seen in the right places with the right people for the right reason. Be a self-starter, go-getter and you will go places.

Things will fall in place after sometime. Until then, you will have to wait.

And finally, remember, your willingness and ability to change and adapt yourself is critical for feeling at home with the new environment.

Your success largely depends on how fast you integrate into the system, connect with people and practices. This will make you feel at home in the new environment. And if you do that you can claim that you are adept to adapt with the environment!

3

COMMUNICATION SKILLS

Expressing yourself better

- Get it right with the basics — Reading, Writing, Speaking
- The Art of Public Speaking
- Presentation Skills
- Technology Aids Communication
- The Seven Cs of Effective Communication

To be a manager is to be a communicator. The person and the function are inextricably interwoven

—Morris E. Massey

Communication Skills are a must for today's executives irrespective of their nature of job. It has become imperative for everyone to be an expert communicator so as to get themselves across, be heard and achieve their objectives. Mastery in communicating what you want helps you to stand out distinctly.

Almost all job ads highlight excellent communication skills as an important criterion for selection. As such, let none be left in doubt that communication skills are very crucial for everyone to survive in the corporate world. It can make or mar your career progress and even fetch you plum jobs. It only underscores the need for executives to master communication skills in order to get ahead.

Let's start with the basics. The process of communication involves at least two people — sender and the receiver.

Communication will be meaningful only when what is said or sent is understood well and the response is relevant. As you know, communication is complete when it is two-way.

Communication is more than mere-reading, writing, speaking and listening. It is intended to bring about a communion of minds. What you communicate must be understood in the same sense by others so as to ensure 'meeting of minds' and 'hearts'. A skilful manager communicates to bring around people to see his point of view or make people fall in line with his decision, not by exercising of his authority but by his power to persuade and to convince. Brevity and clarity are the cornerstones of good communication. Communication break-downs, gaps and lags in communication can be avoided to a great extent if proper channels of communication and modes for transmitting are in place.

Communication is of two types:

1. Verbal Communication (Oral and written)
2. Non-verbal Communication (Body language and gestures)

Communication is described as the glue that holds an organisation together, the very essence of an organisation. In short, communication is a means by which behavior is modified, change is effected, information is made productive and goals are achieved.

Communication skills are of two types:

1. Receptive
2. Productive

In receptive type, you are passive. Reading, listening and understanding constitute receptive communication skills.

In productive type, you are active. Public speaking is an excellent example of this type of communications skills.

There are two essential ingredients of communication:

1. Substance — What you say
2. Style — How you say

Any communication is said to have substance when it conveys the message in a clear and unambiguous manner. All necessary and important points are covered and nothing irrelevant is present. The vocabulary — the choice of words is excellent giving no room for bombastic language.

Style denotes the how you present your thoughts and views in your communication. It is so well structured that you put the right word at the right place.

Communication involves content and language. The stuff should have substance and presenting the same must be done in style. Remember, what you say is as important as how you say.

Consider these sentences,

- "A piano belonging to a lady with 4 ornamental legs is for sale".
- "My friend sold his house over a cup of tea for Rs. 7,50,000".

How did that sound? Clarity, as opposed to ambiguity, is important in communication.

You must have heard of a popular anecdote in management circles how communication gap almost cost the job of a factory worker, for no fault of his. It so happened that a company wanted to offer group insurance to its employees. One clause of the policy specified that in order to be covered by the policy every employee must give his consent to participate. As expected every one signed the insurance papers except one factory worker who was stubborn not to do so. First, his foreman asked him to comply to which he flatly refused. Next came the supervisor who drew a blank. The Factory Manager's attempt was also in vain. At last, the owner called our obstinate friend and said, "Listen you idiot! If you are not signing, I am going to fire you". The worker immediately consented and signed. The astonished owner asked him the reason for his immediate compliance. To which he replied "No one explained it as clearly as you".

Got the message? So be a good communicator leaving none in doubt and half your problems will be solved.

Communication skills, simply refers to your ability to express yourself clearly — be it verbal or written. The ability to convey what you intend to communicate is the key.

According to Wayne Pennington, "The great challenge in communicating is to understand the mind, the background and the thinking process of your audience. If you know these, you can prevent a lot of 'communication static'".

Use simple and short sentences initially. As and when you are comfortable with the language you can start using complex sentences.

Dr. Samuel Johnson, the great English literary figure, was so fond of using bombastic language. Sample these,

"His verticality was reduced to horizontality" for "He fell down"

"Ornithological specimens of identical species are congregated" to mean "Birds of feather flock together"

Many novices in their efforts to communicate overdo the act. One basic ground rule in communication is "Excessive communication is counter-productive". Every so often we find people saying, "He spoke for one hour but he said nothing". So understand that the more you talk the less you communicate.

The Basics of Communication

The success of these three — your marriage, job and relationships with others depends a great deal on your ability to communicate. The following are the basic aspects to be considered in any form of communication.

1. Be positive in your communication
2. Listen to others
3. Put the other person at ease
4. Remove distractions
5. Clarity of thoughts is essential
6. Be brief and upto the point
7. Empathize
8. Avoid communicating when angry
9. Don't argue and criticize

10. Ask direct questions
11. Give necessary information
12. Make your point clear without ambiguity
13. Be clear about the scope of your subject
14. Repeat yourself to get across
15. Try to get response from the listener

In short, if you are able to express your thoughts and feelings, views and opinions without any difficulty in a clear and unambiguous manner I am sure that you have won the first round in your battle for acquiring communication skills.

It's been said that the message is more important than the messenger. Yet for the effective delivery of the message, the messenger should be a top-notch communicator. Else the message, however excellent it may be, will be messed by the messenger.

The Importance of Reading

> Reading is the input; communication is the output. Reading is the main product; communication is the by-product.

To improve your communication skills it is pertinent to be a voracious reader. The more you read the more skills you acquire. Your horizons widen in many ways. Apart from the knowledge you gain about the subject you read, you are exposed to the style of presentation, vocabulary, elegance of language, felicity of expression, etc. But here is a catch. Read high quality literature to improve yourself. Lay your hands on standard magazines and newspapers and read literary classics. The more you read the better. Reading sparks the thinking process. As you get exposed to a variety of topics your horizons widen providing you with a perceptible shift and change in the pattern of thinking. This is critical because the quality of your thoughts determines the quality of your communication. And the real impetus in your efforts — be it communication skills or anything else, come only when you have the ability to think and learn. This ability is the base for improvement in any field.

To communicate effectively you don't have to be necessarily a wordsmith or have scholarly knowledge. Other frills like having your own style of language, vocabulary, felicity of expression, etc aren't much of a problem. If you get it right with the basics then adding other things will be easy. It's just like if you know how to walk you can easily learn running. Over a period of time and with constant learning and practice you can develop these and go on to become an excellent communicator.

Get it Right with the Basics — Reading, Writing, Speaking

Reading maketh a full man,
Conference a ready man and
Writing an exact man

—Francis Bacon

It makes a sad commentary on the sort of education we get these days that the aim of which is solely to get marks, higher marks with no attempt whatsoever to make the taught to acquire basic skills of reading, writing and speaking. Though some people inherently develop these skills but many lag behind due to lack of it. Here, I am discussing the importance of them and how it helps in an executive's career.

READING

Reading maketh the man

Reading is the first step towards learning and acquiring knowledge through self-efforts. For it needs none to coach or lecture us. A good book of our choice is enough to set us on our intellectual pursuit endeavors.

With the advent of television the habit of reading has become almost extinct in kids and grown ups have succumbed to the pressures of work, time and energy.

Reading is considered as windows of your mind. Reading makes use of certain parts of the brain in not just recognizing words but also in understanding the concepts and ideas expressed in a book. When we read a mystery novel we have visualise the scenario and get thrilled or while reading a humorous book we laugh with the hilarity.

However, poor reading techniques are one major reason why people don't prefer to take up reading as a habit. A lack of understanding of the contents in the book may not be your fault. The book's poor presentation may be one reason. While buying books make sure that they are well laid out, indexed, easy to read and comprehend and includes a glossary for your ready reference. See that you feel comfortable with the book and you develop an interest to read its contents. In short, the book must appeal to you.

How to Read?

1. The First Look. Look at the contents section given in the initial pages of the book and this gives you an overall idea about the subject handled. Read the author's note/ Preface or Foreword which further enlightens you about the *raison d'etre* of the book. But never judge a book by the cover.

2. Look for Signposts. Signposts are spots which are easy to attract the reader's attention. They are of two types:

1. Visual Signposts
2. Verbal Signposts

Visual signposts include underlined or italicized or words set in bold face or different font. Bulleted or numbered points, capitalized words and sub-headings also constitute visual signposts.

Verbal signposts are used to introduce important points. The following are some examples:

Verbal Signposts	**Meaning**
1. Firstly, Secondly	Lists details
2. Therefore	A sum up before concluding
3. However	Introduce a qualification
4. For instance	Gives example
5. Moreover/Furthermore	Supports the main idea
6. On the other hand	Contradicts a point
7. Nevertheless	Inspite of that
8. Similarly	Tells about something alike

Techniques for Effective Reading

There are two techniques to make your reading more beneficial.

1. Active Reading. To make your reading session active and purposeful you need to involve yourself in the points made in the book. One possible way is to question critically and then accept the ideas and opinions. You will have a better understanding of the concept. Sift facts from fiction.

2. Visualise. The text should be visualized and related to your own experience. As you read visualise the scenario the author presents and you will start enjoying the book. Correlate reality with the points espoused in the book. Try to compare your experience and see whether they can be applicable or not.

3. Vocalise. To a great extent vocalisation — reading aloud helps readers (beginners) to concentrate on the text without allowing any distractions to creep in. Reading aloud, though appears too naïve for grown ups, yet it is useful to focus the mind on the book when it is difficult. But avoid this technique when in a library or when among a group.

Faster Reading

Faster reading helps to save time and energy.

For beginners the going may be slow yet with practice and training one can increase reading speed considerably. Research suggests that the average reader clocks a speed of 240 words per minute (wpm). With further training, one can attain speeds of about 360 wpm. With sustained effort and practice you can achieve 600 wpm.

While reading faster care must be taken to ensure that you don't suffer from loss of comprehension. Mind you, a trade-off between faster reading and understanding of the content will make the reading exercise meaningless.

You can read fast when the content has details which are familiar, re-emphasising statements and well-known facts. Slow down if the text is unfamiliar, tough vocabulary, lengthy sentences whose meaning is difficult to grasp at the first reading and information is detailed.

Researchers have found that when we read our eyes move in a jerky motion. The brain reads words at each fixation of the eye. Which means you can read only when your eyes stop and this stop is known as fixation. To become a fast reader you must increase you span of recognition.

There are two techniques for rapid reading.

1. **Skipping.** Recognition span will be wide and more when you concentrate to read only the main ideas fixing your eyes at the middle of the sentences. You will, over practice, know what to read and what to skip. Just like how you can fairly tell the last part of a movie by seeing the first part of it. When you become adept in knowing what to overlook you have indeed mastered skipping technique.

2. **Skimming.** In this technique, you are skimming the cream of the content. You don't have to read word by word to get to know the idea. Your recognition span will let you to have a wide glance when you start to read. Skimming technique also involves overlooking unnecessary words. Fast newspaper readers are perfect in using this technique. Just by looking at the headlines and a few sentences of the text they will know the story and they will proceed on to the next item.

People are capable of reading more than 100 pages in 3 hours time. However, faster reading must be employed only in light hearted literature, novels, newspapers and magazines and not for research papers, serious study, etc. However, with persistence in practice one can attain speed without compromising on comprehension.

How to Gain most of Reading?

1. **Read with a purpose.** Always read with a purpose. Reading a book needs concentration of the mind. It is not a causal reading like magazines and newspapers. Reading is a serious. Define what for you need to read and next what to read.

2. **Stumbling blocks?** Don't expect to understand whatever you read in first attempt. Whenever you come across a stumbling block, skip over it after marking it with some visual signpost. Come back to it after you consult a good dictionary.

3. **Dictionary as your personal teacher.** Keep a good dictionary handy. You can learn a lot by referring to it. A

dictionary goes beyond giving the meaning of words. If you carefully notice a word you can see how it is pronounced, whether it is British or American, its usage supplemented with an example and which part of speech. A dictionary is a mine of information in these respects.

4. Gain something out of reading. Read a book to gain something out of it. Not for mere time-pass. As I said before don't give a cursory treatment as you give to the newspaper. Even with a good newspaper you can learn not merely get to know the news. Make it a point to observe the style and elegance of language, the vocabulary, narrative style, presentation techniques, quotations, etc. Also note the author of the write-up so that as you gain experience by reading regularly you can even make out the author by seeing their style of writing.

5. Create your own knowledge bank. Reading must be intensive. If you want to make most out of your reading, you must develop the habit of taking notes in a sheet of paper. Human memory is so short-lived that 80% of what you read will be forgotten within 24 hours. Within a week's time 90% will be forgotten and eventually almost everything. Then you will have only a vague memory of what you read. Now do you remember last Monday's headline in the newspaper? So take notes of quotations and sayings which appeal you most, as you read. Keep the paraphernalia handy. If the article which impresses you most is lengthy, cut and file them neatly with index for future references. This way you can develop your own personal knowledge bank, if not a library.

Benefits of Reading

Soak yourself with the world's best literature,
so that you will have words, strong words,
clear words for your speaking.

—Dr. L.H. Hough

Reading fires your imagination, kindles your thirst for knowledge. It helps us to indulge in intellectual gymnastics — broadens our horizons and outlook. Reading a good book will be equivalent of having conversation with the finest of men. It is like travelling in time with a new experience in every page without moving a foot forward.

Read extensively. Without leaving the threshold of your home, with the aid of a book your mind can travel to the Grand Canyon, Taj Mahal, Eiffel Tower or just wherever you want. They all come alive in the pages of the book. Reading travelogues, popularly known as armchair-travelling, takes you on a world tour just having to spend for the cost of the book. Also you can take an escape from today's fast-paced world by getting into a time warp and witness the battles of Alexander, the glory of the Roman Empire, the World Wars or just anything you like. The value of reading and the effect it has on one's mind is to be experienced. Words cannot explain the joy one gets out of it.

In short, the benefits of reading are listed below:

1. Gain knowledge
2. Broadens your horizons and outlook.
3. Useful and less-expensive pastime
4. Builds vocabulary, style of writing, elegance of language.
5. Helps you to express your thoughts better.
6. Reading is fun.
7. Makes you happy and glad to sit in a quiet corner with a good book in hand.

Further, reading is intricately woven with speaking. Read what Hoffman says how extensive reading helps in speaking well,

> "Men who talk well read more, as a rule, than the average. Without conscious effort, they absorb many ideas and the words that express them.... Reading is considered the most potent single factor in the enlargement of vocabulary".

The Joy of Reading

If you look at the annals of history you will find that everyone who is considered as an intellectual giant was at, one point or other, a voracious reader.

Louis L'Amour, writer of frontier adventures became so enamored of books that he came to own 9000 of them.

"Once you discover how much fun it can be to read", he says, "life is never dull, and the interest grows with each book. My library is Aladdin's lamp. I can, at will, move into any time of history. I can talk with the great minds of the past with philosophers, outlaws, cattlemen, adventurers, with kings, queens and common sailors. It is all there waiting for me".

Continues L'Amour,

> "It is often said that one has but one life to live, but that is nonsense. For one who reads, there is no limit to the number of lives that may be lived, for fiction, biography and history offer an inexhaustible number of lives in many parts of the world, in all periods of time".

So get set to make reading part of your daily schedule.

WRITING

Think before you ink

Writing is a form of expression of your thoughts and ideas. It is a skill which needs to be practiced before you become perfect. Just because you are proficient in one or more languages you cannot become a writer straight away. Overnight success cannot be expected while you are about to write. You must be a voracious reader first. You should have thorough, if not scholarly, knowledge in the subject you want to deal with. Then you must have the ability to put in your own words what you feel, structuring your thoughts in a logical sequence and put them in writing that is easy for others to understand.

Good writers have made it possible through their writings that it is no way inferior to public speaking. Unlike public speakers, writers have many advantages. First, they can write taking their own time to finish a write-up. They are not constrained by the limitations imposed by time, place and energy. Secondly, written word is more powerful and has longevity. It is said that "Pen is mightier than the sword". History is replete with instances of writers who have been able, through the charm and power of their writings, to start revolts, bring down governments and cause revolutions. Such is the power of writing that in your career people would be able to notice you if you are proficient enough to put down your views vividly and that is easy to follow.

A writer must do in ink what an artist does in oils — pick out the significant, make it interesting and appealing.

Aims of a Good Write-up

1. Your write-up should be absorbing, thought-provoking and interesting.
2. Readers should be able to comprehend what you write. Use simple language.
3. Writing aims to express your views in a clear manner free from ambiguity.
4. It needn't be conventional. Writers can adopt any style of writing.

Before You Write

1. Be clear as to what you intend to write.
2. Assemble your thoughts in a linear fashion.
3. Collect facts and figures to supplement your main story.
4. Provide examples and quotations to spice up your write-up.
5. Know when to stop writing.

After You Write

1. Check and re-check your write-up for mistakes — grammatical, spelling, punctuation.
2. Ensure your facts and figures and other statistical information are correct.
3. Delete irrelevant items and keep your write-up upto the point.
4. Check your examples and quotations so as to make them relevant to the point you make.
5. Provide the finishing touch by giving an effective sum up at the end.

Writing is a gift of God. Use it judiciously for the welfare of others, for a just cause and in short, for the well-being of mankind. Don't write anything intending to hurt people. It cannot be withdrawn, however much you regret it later. It's been said that "The art of writing is the art of restraint". Most of the people however, educated and qualified they may be, can write to impress. A skilful copy and paste job cannot bring everlasting success and glory. Only the chosen few who know the pulse of their readers can write by expressing genuinely from their heart and they can enjoy universal acclaim and honor. Read on to know Mahatma Gandhi's views on writing,

> "To be true to my faith, therefore, I may not write in anger or malice. I may not write idly. I may not write merely to excite passion. The reader can have no idea of the restraint I have to exercise from week to week in the choice of topics and vocabulary. It is training for me. It enables me to peep into myself and to make discoveries of my weaknesses. Often my vanity dictates a smart expression or my anger a harsh adjective. It is a terrible ordeal but a fine exercise to remove these weeds".
>
> —M.K. Gandhi; *Young India*, July 2, 1925

Business Writing

Business writing consists, among others, of writing business letters and reports. Follow this principle in all your written communication: "Think before you ink".

Guidelines for Business Communication

1. Long reports should be divided into paragraphs each conveying one point/topic.
2. If possible, put your points numbering them consecutively or bullet them.
3. Group each topic under a sub heading.
4. Underline or make important points bold.
5. Be brief, but brevity should not be traded off for clarity.
6. Conclude by giving a brief sum up and state clearly what you want.

7. Write letters that are short and brief aiming to interest readers, capture their attention, win their approval and get desired action.
8. The writer needn't have to display his depth of learning. He must have the ability to correlate and co-ordinate facts and present them in an attractive manner.
9. While writing remember that the target of your write-up, be it a business letter or report, is a person and not a situation. You will have to interpret your thoughts to your readers who view the world not in terms of facts but also of personalities and emotions.
10. Ensure that you don't misrepresent facts. For it may cost your reputation and it will be expensive. Be accurate and research well before you put it down writing.
11. A written business communication needs your personal attention. Don't think that a good stenographer would take care. At best, he can ensure spelling, grammar and neat presentation in appropriate stationery. It falls on your part to fill up the main stuff.
12. Consider before penning things that concern the reader, his level of comprehension, his present understanding of the subject and the kind of language that will be appropriate for the occasion.
13. Don't write anything when you are angry.
14. Write to communicate, to inform and don't use bombastic language. Avoid jargon as much as possible.
15. A well-structured business report or letter will achieve your objectives. It all depends on the presentation you make.

It must be agreed that all good writers are basically and essentially thinkers but the same may not hold good for thinkers because they may not be good writers. There is immense power in thinking and a writer gets his ideas from deep contemplation. As such aspiring writers must learn to think objectively, structuring their thoughts well so as to put them in writing.

Speaking

Don't speak all you think. But think all you speak

Speaking is the most familiar, easy and natural way of communication which we all do since our birth. But at many a time, people get caught in the wrong foot due to a few lapses. The following aspects are to be considered while talking with others:

1. A strong foundation. Before you speak you must have some command over the language you are going to use. Mind your pronunciation and accent. To the maximum possible extent ensure that your accent doesn't betray your mother-tongue or region. Speak in an accent which is neutral and free from any influences.

2. Speak with confidence. When you speak with confidence you are bound to be heard seriously. People take interest in what you say and your image grows in their eyes. Mind you, your confidence level is easy for others to find out for your tone and energy levels of your conversation betray it.

3. Think twice before you speak. Never speak without forethought. For words which are spoken cannot be recalled. Speak in such a way that it will not affect or hurt others. But speak the truth. Speak truth when it is pleasant and will benefit people. Think of the implications your talk will produce before you open your mouth. Be a diplomat.

4. Make eye-contact. This is one aspect most people, irrespective of their level of education and qualification choose to ignore. Speaking without making eye-contact may have one of the following reasons:

(a) Not confident while speaking.

(b) Afraid to meet the other person eye-to-eye.

(c) Just plain ignorance.

(d) Dislike for the listener.

So look people in the eye when you speak.

5. Avoid mono-syllables. Another common mistake people do is the habit of answering in mono-syllables. People expect you to be clear and articulate. They don't like to get reply in mono-syllables. It shows you in poor light if you answer in mono-syllables. It means that either you don't have the confidence to speak or you don't like to talk or you lack good communication skills.

6. Be sincere, direct and objective. Sincerity and seriousness have no alternatives while speaking. Be genuine in your words. Let your enthusiasm show. Speak with an objective. Structure your talk so as to drive home the points you intend to make. Don't ramble and rave aimlessly. Come to the point directly instead of being roundabout and it will save time — yours and others.

7. Avoid sarcasm, name-dropping and jargon. Sarcastic manner of your talk easily makes listeners to lose interest in you and it also portrays you as person who is critical with malice. As they say, "Sarcasm is humor that has lost its patience". Also avoid name-dropping though it seems to be fashionable. It doesn't enhance your image, rather it projects you as a man of straw.

Clarity of speech and thought is necessary. Avoid jargon and make your talk which is easy to understand. Detest from using bombastic and high-sounding words. If you continue to do so, people will brand you as a follower of latest fads and not as you would like to be.

8. Don't bully. Never think you can get things your way by bullying or speaking in a coercive manner. Threats will work only for sometime and not in the long run. Don't shout down or talk down your subordinates. Be persuasive and people would listen to you more. Remember that logic is more powerful than force.

9. Speak naturally. Another common mistake people make is to hide their natural accent and try to imitate others — film stars, politicians, sport stars, etc. You cannot be what you are not. Speak in a natural manner but it doesn't mean that you should not improve your pronunciation and accent. Do it but don't imitate blindly.

10. Interact. Hold listener interest by asking questions, calling people by their names, titles, etc. Punctuate your speech with interesting facts, anecdotes and pepper with humor. Give the other person enough chance to express his views. Every now and then, pause for a moment so as to elicit response from the listener. Or else it will be a boring monologue. Speaking or for that matter communication is a two-way street. Allow people to interact with you to know what they have in their minds without fear or favor.

11. Voice matters. Speak with a steady voice. Don't be loud or talk in whispers. Both irritate people. Modulate your voice to emphasise and make a point. A monotonous drone will easily put people off. Neither speak fast nor slow. Moderate your pace on an even speed.

12. Gesture. Even in a one-to-one talk gestures and body language matter a lot. They supplement what you say. When you speak use appropriate gestures to emphasise and they go down well and at times they are more powerful than words.

Stop Talking! Start Listening!

We hear with our ears. We listen with our minds

Listening Skills are imperative to know and understand other's view points. We all hear others and but seldom listen. Hearing and listening are different. When we watch news on the TV, we hear a lot many sounds like the whirring of the fan or purring of the AC but we listen intently to the newsreader. Similarly in our business communication with people, we merely hear their voice instead of listening to them.

Listen to understand. Listening is complete when you understand what the other person says.

We don't listen when we are:

1. Tired and exhausted
2. Angry
3. Biased and have prejudices
4. Not in better frame of mind (like arriving late to a meeting)
5. Lose interest in the speaker
6. Trying to say something
7. Pre-occupied with some thought in our mind

8. Not well
9. We don't like the source.
10. Simply, not prepared to listen

Be a Good Listener First

"The best listener is someone who puts himself in the other person's shoes".

You can be a good listener and benefit by doing the following:

1. Concentrate. Focus the mind on the speaker by clearing out all other thoughts. This way you tune in your listening antenna. You become receptive.

2. Give cues and prompts. Show that you are listening by giving appropriate vocal cues. Punctuate your silence by saying 'yes', 'fine', 'good', etc.

3. Be attentive. Don't let your mind to wander away. Also keep an open mind. Don't make assumptions and listen carefully to what the other person says.

4. Avoid interrupting. Give the other person the chance to finish what he intends to say. Never say no until you have heard fully.

5. Be patient. Have patience until the other person finishes. Don't give the impression that you are impatient.

6. Clarify. If you don't understand, stop to clarify. Never pretend to understand. It can be disastrous. Stop the speaker then and there for such clarifications. Don't embarrass him by letting him to finish and finally asking to repeat all over again.

7. Use body language. Listening doesn't mean only to hear the words. Use positive body language so as to encourage the speaker to carry on.

8. Don't appear to judge. Don't sound judgemental until you hear fully. If you persist so, you won't get to know the correct picture and you may cloud the mind of the other person with your personal bias and prejudice.

9. Ask open questions to encourage the speaker to continue.

Don't believe all you hear. Judge others' talk objectively. Never believe instantly of people who take extreme positions. There is more to it than what the ear hears.

One constant complaint from subordinates against their bosses is that they don't listen to whatever they say. In many cases, bosses are in no mood to hear at all what his subordinate is saying. They never give a chance to speak and communication is only one-way. Seldom do we find bosses who lend a patient ear and they are the ones who are sensible. Bear in mind, your staff are close to the customers or markets and since they are in the field they know better than you! So make up your mind to give a patient hearing the next time they meet you.

You have greater impact on others by the way you listen than by the way you talk.

As the saying goes, to speak is to sow; to listen is to reap.

By listening intently, you will understand better as to what the other person is saying. Also you can notice his attitude well and form an image about him in your mind. Facts and details hitherto unknown will emerge and flash only if you care to listen.

In fact, all effective communication starts with listening! So stop talking and start listening. And good communicators are at first good listeners!

Are you listening?

The Art of Public Speaking

If all my possessions were taken from me, with one exception, I would choose to keep the power of speech, for by it, I would soon regain all the rest.

—Daniel Webster

I hope you will agree with me when I say that one of the top ten fundamental human terrors is making a public speech. Just ask and see how many of your colleagues (include yourself too) are willing to do it. For any professional irrespective of the nature of the jobs they perform, a time arises when they have to speak before a group of individuals, familiar or not. Here is where people will have to invest some time and energy in developing that wonderful art called public speaking.

One-to-one communication is easy and normal for any human being. But one-to-many communication requires some guts and special skills which you can develop over a period of time if not over night!

The executive who is an expert in public speaking will present a picture of confidence and capable of handling any assignment entailing oratory duties. He will not shirk from such responsibilities since he knows the value of such opportunities. For opportunities do not come your way regularly. Public speaking opportunities are not to be missed at any cost since it helps you to project your image before a group of audience. Moreover such chances come once in a blue moon and rarely frequent unless your profession demands it. Taking advantage of public speaking opportunities is useful in presenting yourself in a different facet hitherto unknown to many, even to people close to you.

A good public speaker will possess excellent communication skills, command of language and put forth his ideas and opinions clearly free from ambiguity.

There are very few simple prerequisites to become a good public speaker. Firstly, you must love to meet different people particularly over a group of individuals. Secondly, you must develop fearlessness and courage and have the passion to talk. Clarity of thought and speech are other factors to be taken care of. Other skills can be acquired steadily with constant practice.

The Aims of Public Speaking

To speak is to communicate. But public speaking goes beyond this basic function. It utilizes communication with a specific purpose to a group of people. Public speaking aims to:

1. Inform
2. Persuade
3. Negotiate
4. Inspire

No wonder, public speaking is also a performing art. When you look at the annals of history, it is the oratory skills of people which made leaders out of common man. Right from Mark Antony to Winston Churchill to today's political leaders have used their public speaking skills to the hilt in getting to the top. Ancient Greece and Rome were famed for many rabble-rousing speakers who made the audience to dance to their tunes making them to cry or laugh at their will and pleasure. People-commoners and kings alike valued public speakers. Dictators even fear those people. Even the German Fuhrer Adolf Hitler so effectively manipulated the crowd that they listened to him in rapt attention for one...two...three... perhaps for hours together hypnotized by his charms and power of public speaking.

Such is the effect of public speaking that the executive who is adept at it can have his audience to eat out of his palms and make it clamor for more. He wields the power of persuasion and can convince people with ease. The power of public speaking is so effective that the speaker, at the movement of tongue can sway the audience.

Public Speaking Types

The result of public speaking is of two types:

1. Appealing to logic.
2. Appealing to psychology.

The first type leaves the audience to ponder and contemplate in solitude and peace and then act accordingly. It appeals to thinking, intellect and reason. The language used will be thought-provoking and it aims to set people thinking and draw their own conclusions in a passive way. The audience will nod approvingly and clap in appreciation.

In the second type, the speech is powerful and rabble-rousing that the audience soon after hearing would just be spurred into action. It appeals to the listeners' feelings, emotions and sentiments directly. Here the speech is not a passive affair. It is fire. Speech is the cause of action though it is not an alternative to action. Most politicians, military leaders and religious zealots follow this style of public speaking.

Benefits of Learning Public Speaking Skills

Some of the benefits that accrue from learning, developing and perfecting public speaking skills are listed below:

1. Improves clarity of expression.
2. Coordinates thought and speech.
3. Builds confidence.
4. Provides an exit vent for dispensing your ideas and opinion.
5. Enhances articulating skills.
6. Expands your vocabulary, language and ultimately gives command over the language.
7. Enlarges your mental horizons and awareness level.

Agree or not, but one fact which stands out is that all teachers are, by their own right, more or less, public speakers. Either by conscious self-effort induced training or by nature they hold the attention of students at most times a bunch of unruly, boisterous and undisciplined lot. By a blend of verbal and non-verbal communication they sought to teach, inform and at times to inspire students. However, in their cases, the audience was familiar and they had the authority to back up. But for a public speaker the situation is difficult altogether. Public speakers are at home both with familiar audiences and unknown people. They capture the hearts of audience by storm with their erudition, poise, charm, delivery and choice of words.

It is not as easy as you think like a guy just with lots of raw guts coming before a group and shouting all he wants to say and getting away with that. A lot number of soft skills need to be mastered.

Anyone can become Public Speaker

Some of the greatest public speakers of the past have at one point of time been plagued by awful stammering. Demosthenes of ancient Greece was one. By sheer practice and hard work, he overcame this physical disability so well that he attained dizzying heights of fame and fortune with his public speaking prowess.

A famous scientist was on his way to yet another lecture when his chauffeur offered an idea. “Hey, boss, I’ve heard your speech so many times, I bet I could deliver it and give you the night off”.

“Sounds great”, the scientist said.

When they got to the auditorium, the scientist put on the chauffeur’s hat and settled into the back row. The chauffeur walked to the dais and delivered the speech. Afterwards he asked if there were any questions.

“Yes”, said one professor. Then he launched into a highly technical question.

The chauffeur was panic-stricken for a moment but quickly recovered. “That’s an easy one”, he replied. “So easy, I’m going to let my chauffeur answer it”.

Well, it was a close call and not everyone would be lucky and get away like him. The point however to be noted is that anyone having the will and ability can master public speaking skills. If he can do, why not you?

Why skills?

Mere will to deliver a speech is not enough. I once attended a convention where a chance was given to the audience to address their views. One guy got up enthusiastically and walked upto the podium briskly. Hardly had he attempted to speak when he was at a loss of how to express them. In broken phrases he tried to put forth his ideas. The points he sought to put before us were solid and meaningful. But he lacked other skills, what is known as soft skills to get across. His raw confidence brought him on to the dais when none dared but it was without soft skills whatsoever which proved to be his undoing and he ran away in embarrassment with an entire hall jeering and roaring with laughter. It was ironic that the guy chose to speak on the topic of public speaking! He had the confidence to come forward to address a hall of perhaps thousand students and the stuff. But the absence of soft skills was apparent.

It was like desiring to drive a car without driving skills but knowing well the route to the destination.

The Skills you Need

Good public speakers possess soft skills which aim at making themselves endearing to the audience they address. Soft skills for a public speaker help him in mastering the nuances of putting forth his views, opinions and ideas in a very subtle way. Remember that there are many ways to get the message home other than just with the mouth. Verbal communication is greatly complemented by non-verbal communication.

Before the Event

Before the speech you will have to do your home work well.

- Know your topic well in advance
- Familiarize with the venue
- Prepare your topic well
- Perfect the diction
- Rehearse, rehearse, rehearse
- Prepare your speech to finish within the allotted time
- Be prepared for any contingency
- Know something about group psychology

Speech writing is an art in itself which is as important as the public speaking skills. Not many can prepare their own speeches and a special kind of writers abound known as speech writers. However, discussing in detail about this art is beyond the scope of this book.

Train up Your Voice

Your voice should be loud and clear just as the message you seek to send across. The speaker must be loud but not like a loud speaker. By loudness I mean, audibility and not shouting. A strong tone as opposed to a shaky one would help in getting the attention of your audience. Clear your throat before you start speaking. If the going gets tough, slow down and recover your poise. If you cannot speak for long without taking a few sips of water, inform in advance to the organizers to provide you with water placed at arms length. Excuse yourself for a moment to the audience and drink without making noise quickly and return to where you left off. However, it is not in the best interest of the speech you are making and hence try to avoid such interruptions.

Squeaky voice or voice that is troubled by coughs and grunts do not go well with the listeners. A feeble voice means that the speaker is not confident and is afraid to proceed further and a gruff voice will not feel nice to be heard. A booming voice may not be fine in a formal setting. What you say must not only be audible but also have the clarity. Don't speak too fast or too slow.

Rehearse prior to the actual event with the help of a tape recorder. Replay it a number of times to hear how it feels to you. Improve upon it accordingly. Successful public speakers possess strong and resonant voice that ring in the ears of the audience well after the speech is over.

Have Commitment

Before accepting to give a speech think well as to whether you can live up to your promise. Have commitment towards your job and when you agree to speak honor it in all ways possible. People invest their time, energy and come all the way to hear you and if you are a celebrity even money. And you don't have the right to let them down. Never cancel your speech unless it is absolutely necessary and unavoidable. In such eventuality, at least have the courtesy to inform well in advance so that the organizers make alternate arrangements without going red-faced.

Be Punctual

This is one important personal quality that every one in general and in this context, public speakers, in particular, must possess. Being late for a speech that too when you are the main speaker is not a symbol of eminence while it may be fine in a social party though the practice is questionable. Public speakers should be punctual as gentlemen do not like to be kept waiting.

In order to take the sting out of such ignominious apology do it imaginatively with an amusing reason and the audience will marvel at your ability to turn a lapse on your part into an advantage.

MOMENTS PRIOR TO SPEECH

Managing your Emotions

A range of emotions will envelope you at those crucial moments. Learning to manage and take charge of your emotions and physical responses is the first success you will achieve before you proceed to deliver your speech. At first the going will be tough. The very scene of yourself standing before a thousand unfamiliar faces which stares back at you may be unnerving initially. You see a multitude of faces at the first glance without seeing anyone in particular but see everyone in general.

Before you start the speech your body undergoes a lot of biological reactions due to emotional feelings like fear, anxiety, etc. Experienced speakers don't face such problems but beginners are susceptible. Pre-speech nerves leave your body flushing with adrenalin. Your body responds in various ways in what can be termed as 'Stage Fear' like profuse sweating, heart pounding, quivering voice, breathing trouble, butterflies-in-the-stomach feeling which are easy for the audience to find out. A better frame of mind, a confident heart and mastery of the subject will help you to get over these physical inconsistencies.

Smile

The warmth of a smile can light up a person's day

—Rabbi Moshe Goldberger

Smile when you enter the hall. People will respond or at least it will spread an air of goodwill across the hall. It will generate the feel-good factor and the audience will like it. It is no surprise to know that a smile effectively puts out those thought waves among the audience who may be hostile to you or your ideas. Also it can help in warding off negative influences emanating from the audience. So smile and let it be infectious.

A smile is the only gesture with which the speaker initially tries to create a rapport with the audience. It works. Let your smile be as natural as possible. If your cheeks begin to ache due to forced smile then you are putting on a false smile. Try to smile all through the speech and while doing so don't do it so glaringly that people take you for posing for a tooth paste advertisement.

Before Taking the Plunge

A certain level of tension is necessary to make you give your optimum. So don't worry much about such tensions. Even experienced orators put up with such tensions.

Walk into the hall briskly and it shows you as a person of confidence. A slow and unsteady swagger will lower your esteem among your audience. Remember first impression is the best impression. So never commit any blunders during those initial crucial moments or else it is difficult to gain the lost ground.

The first few minutes are very crucial and within those moments you need to create a powerful impression with the audience and win over them. The audience is very shrewd and clever for they will in a minute size up what kind of person you are and find your caliber. You must also try to gauge the audience mood by one glance which gives a sweeping view of the entire hall.

Before starting a speech, take a few deep breaths audible only to you, to drain away the built up tension. Compose yourself. Don't get agitated when you hear your name announced repeatedly or when finding the mike singing its own tune. Be cool. Clear your throat, if necessary. Adjust the mike and request to turn away the arc lights if they are too glaring. Stand in a position that leaves a good distance between the lips and tip of the mike. If it would help, send a silent prayer to heaven and take the plunge headlong.

Starting the Speech

With a silent prayer you will find fresh confidence and courage. Address the audience and organizer with appropriate salutations, introduce yourself, if necessary, with your name, your background and the purpose of the speech you are about to make. And all these are to happen within a couple of minutes and not more. Also remember to thank the organizer for giving you the opportunity to speak.

If you find the atmosphere tense or gloomy, start off with a hearty joke so that you involve everyone and make them to hear you. Humor eases the situation and is a key to establish rapport with the audience.

During the initial moments, start speaking slowly and once you assess your audience as to whether they are able to keep pace with you and follow, then increase your speed steadily. But this is not required for familiar audiences.

Soft Skills

Some of the soft skills and other factors that will aid a speaker are discussed below:

1. **Dress.** Dress appropriately for the occasion. Don't sport flashy costumes as they will steal the attention rather than your speech. Formal wear is the usual attire. Casuals are a strict no-no unless the audience is very close and familiar to you and the setting is an informal one. Casual wear sends the message that you are not serious about the task you are about to perform.

Perhaps you may be knowing of this anecdote of how a famous celebrity was once invited to speak at a posh venue, probably, a five-star hotel. Glad to receive the invite, this speaker went to the gates only to be turned back by the guard. The latter wouldn't let go our friend just because he didn't look professional. The speaker tried to explain that he was the chief guest! But it cut no ice with him and the harried speaker had to rush home, change into different attire and only then allowed inside! For he had all along been wearing casuals! So don't take chances and to avoid cutting a sorry figure, dress yourself in formals. Sport a professional look.

Wear the dress with which you are comfortable and used to. Don't try out new and fashionable ones for they make you very self-conscious all through your speech hindering you from giving your best. And the results of which can be disastrous.

2. **Posture.** Have a dignified posture. Conduct yourself with dignity all through Sit straight and while standing to address stand your full height.

3. **Gestures.** Gestures are important and they have to be appropriate to the point you make. They complement your

words. At times, right and proper gestures help in expressing more than what you can do through words. I hope you have seen novices fidgeting, playing with objects like pen, hanky, etc., rocking uncontrollably, clasping tightly their palms, putting their hands into trouser pockets, or worse still scratching their heads. Well, all these are normal for an amateur and it may be difficult to get over these aberrations but with constant practice one may overcome it. One effective way is to stand in front of a full-length mirror and make your speech before an imaginary audience. Watch your gestures and body language so that you can rectify them. Don't make your first live attempt an experiment.

Avoid looking at your watch since people would think that you are in a hurry and they are not important. Glance discreetly to keep track of time.

Research has shown that the contribution of words is as low as 7%, while the tone of the voice constitutes about 38% while the body language a staggering 55%. So realize how important body language is. Nevertheless, the power of words cannot be downplayed. Anyway, what is a speech without words?

4. Eye contact. Maintain eye contact with your audience all through the speech. Unfortunately, this important factor is glossed over by many wannabe speakers who are afraid to do so. Eye-behavior is important. Having eye contact with your audience will help in establishing a silent but powerful rapport with the audience. Just imagine how it would look like if your boss looks at the ceiling or the wall beyond and explains his ideas when making a presentation. Distribute your attention equally among the audience. Sweep the entire hall with your eyes as you speak.

5. Voice modulation. This is nothing but lowering and raising your voice when making your speech according to the point you make. This will help in reviving audience interest and holding it. The tone plays a key role in voice modulation. Can you think of a speech without voice modulation? It will be monotonous and within a few minutes the hall will be echoing your own voice with no audience to listen.

6. Language. The language you use counts much and it has to be decided with the audience to whom you are going to address in mind. When I talk about language it connotes two different meanings:

Firstly, it refers to the language with which you are proficient and fluent. Choose the language with which you are comfortable and deliver a speech confidently. Secondly, it indicates the style you are going to employ in your talk.

Your language style must be simple and easy to understand. Don't use bombastic and high flying words and phrases. On paper it may look good but while listening it may not make sense. So, use simple, understandable words in your speech and avoid altogether the use of jargon and legal terms. You must have heard people saying words repeatedly phrases like, "I mean", "What I am trying to say is", "because", "is nothing but", "Actually", "Catch my point?", "Understood?" etc. Realise the awkwardness of such words and phrases and learn to avoid them in your speeches. People blunder into using such words since they lack confidence or cannot structure the flow of words in speeches properly and it becomes a bad habit difficult to shake off.

Also, clear pronunciation is necessary to make your speech understandable. Get your phonetics right. Improve upon the delivery and diction further. Don't use words which are difficult to pronounce that makes it still tougher to understand. Another point to remember is to be conscious of your accent. Adopt an accent which is neutral permitting none to find out your mother-tongue or the region from where you hail from. Improvement of accent comes from constant practice and keen observation of successful public speakers.

OTHER SKILLS

Keep no Notes

Reading from a prepared text doesn't portray you in best picture. Use notes only when absolutely necessary like quoting long passages or statistics, etc. It shows that you are not confident of expressing your ideas without the aid of notes. Poor memory and stage fear are some of the chief reasons for holding notes. Avoid it as much as possible. Also, it is a hindrance from making an effective eye contact with your audience. They just think what is the fun in giving a speech reading from a paper right from the word go till the end. It is as simple as anyone delivering the speech since all he needs to do is just read everything from the paper. Finally they belittle your efforts and the speech would not go well with them however meaningful may be the points you raise or excellent may be your pronunciation and delivery.

Keep your Speech short — Be Time Conscious

Unfortunately for the audience there are some speakers drone off lengthy speeches which are mostly boring. You will be knowing how it feels when speaker after speaker impose on you long speeches which hold no interest to you. Be brief and don't over do the explanation part. Also don't repeat the points as if your audience is a bunch of school kids. For they are very wise when it comes to observing and criticizing.

These speakers most commonly politicians and union leaders in organisations just don't want to leave hold of the mike as the opportunity is not a frequent one. They will have to be prompted repeatedly either by small notes or ringing bells and the speeches go on well beyond the scheduled time limit. Only when they leave the mike the audience heaves a sigh of relief. Avoid making such mistakes. If you would have observed most business leaders never do this error. Try to follow them. Be time-conscious and finish your speech well within the allotted time. Know the value of time and keep your speech short so that it is high on points and will be appreciated by one and all. However, don't trade off brevity for clarity in your speech.

Stick to the Point

Many speakers mostly those succumbed to the vagaries of old age drift away from the point and wander far off. The audience is at a loss to know why totally irrelevant topics are being dragged into the present lecture. These speakers due to deep engrossed in telling their ideas that they soon lose track of their objectives. Or if the speaker has the grace to know that he has digressed much, he tries to tie up the point he is making with the original story line making it meaningless and disjointed. Starting somewhere and ending up somewhere is not a proper way to make a good speech.

Stick to the point and don't get carried away by all the thousand thoughts that cross your mind in a minute. Also in your endeavor to put across your point don't quote irrelevant examples and dry jokes.

Keep Personal References to the Minimum

It is not a good practice to refer yourself frequently in your speeches. Only famous celebrities dare to do it for they have an image which is a larger than life. Moreover, people have come to hear what you got to say on the subject and not your personal stories eulogizing yourself. However to make your speech interesting and colorful or to reinforce a point, a personal experience or two will help. Speakers who are obsessed without letting go of the opportunity to speak about themselves are crass egoists hell bent on self-boosting their image. It tarnishes their image badly. Their "I-Me-Myself" attitude is evident for all to see.

Watch your Attitude

Your attitude is the first thing that people will notice, whether you are aware or not. So be careful about what you say. Human nature is such that when given an opportunity to boss over others it begins to show off in true colors. And this nature is more apparent when you are the speaker having a mike through which you can bombard the audience for one hour or so. No! That's not the way...not the right attitude. Your arrogance is more evident when you have the chance to speak over a group of people. Be humility personified. This quality is easily noticeable by the way you interact with people during the course of speech and deal with distractions. Anything you want to get done do so politely in a humble way. For the moment the audience detect something amiss with your attitude be sure that things would go wrong or at least your speech isn't much of a success.

Public Speaking is a Two-way Street

You will agree when I say that communication is meaningful only when it is a two-way street. Public speaking also belongs to the same genre and as such the speaker must involve his audience. The moment you get hold of the mike, if you are going to make it out and out your show with no audience response it would be drab and boring. If you are not that skilful be sure that it would be only a matter of time before you discover people snoring off.

May be someone said of boring professors "Professors are speakers who are programmed to speak for one hour". And they may be the ones we are talking about — monotonous and droning.

So look out for occasions in the course of your speech to involve the audience. The first opportunity would come when you make the salutation. When you say "Good Morning" make them to greet you in return. In the first attempt, apparently none cares but repeat the same salutation a bit louder and you are sure to get the loudest response. This is one way to test how your audience is attentive and also apart from your brisk walk and benign smile these first words is going to build the rapport further. The effect is tremendous and beneficial in more than one way. Now the audience will get alert, if sleeping sit up and take notice. They will take neither chances with you nor grow nonchalant with your speech. Having got them to respond at the outset you can be sure that none misses out anything you say and they will hang upon your lips.

Make them Say Yes-yes

Get them to say yes-yes by posing intelligent questions which gives them the option to answer either yes or no. It involves them and they feel happy to participate and answer your questions. You will be only too glad to hear them say yes-yes to all you say and it is one way to make the audience eating out of your palms. But desist attempting this in your initial sessions since the audience will easily see through you and say that you are trying to act too smart.

Your Speech should be Lively

You can make your speech session as lively as possible. Such a session will be obviously noisy and you need to hone your crowd management skills. Some idea about group psychology will be of immense help. Your stature and words must have the power to bring order out of chaos, silence out of din. Lively speakers are more popular with the people.

Have Sense of Humor

Pepper your speech with humorous anecdotes and people will love to attend your speeches. To be humorous doesn't mean you are not serious. It needs special skills to master so as to make it effective. But ensure that you don't over do it since it would wean the speech away from its intended objectives. If you do so, the message you seek to drive home wouldn't go but only the jokes you told. Finally people would say that your speech lacks stuff but full of wit. Don't let your speech to be hijacked by humor and make it become a humor session. Experienced speakers have their audience in splits by interjecting their speech with a keen sense of wit and humor and at the same time see that they make their points. And doing it that way is not everyone can do.

A lively and interactive session will make you and your audience lose track of time and this is one good technique when you feel that the time allotted is too short. The clamoring crowd is enough to make the organizers to let you go on and on.

Listen to Your Audience

While making a speech how do you listen to your audience? It is possible. By listening to your audience I mean, knowing the pulse of the audience by their reactions. Just as how the speaker uses facial expressions and body language in a speech the audience too responds with them. A good speaker will listen to his audience response and find out the general mood.

Different facial expressions and gestures like shifting of legs, wringing of palms, disinterested looks, squirming in the seats, tapping of the foot, etc., indicate the mood of the crowd. You can accordingly adapt your speech and get along well with the crowds. So have a sharp lookout for such gestures and be intelligent in interpreting them.

Silence too Helps

Silence, surprisingly, helps in a speech. A well-timed pause will help in making your ideas sink in the minds of the audience and they will appreciate it. Don't ramble on like a super fast express train. Pause when necessary and let the audience to ponder.

Be Prepared for any Eventuality

It happens at times that the audience mood is bad and the speech you make doesn't go well with them. Or there are some pranksters hell bent on creating mischief and distracting your attention. Or a crying baby disturbs your speech. Distractions for the speaker come in galore. A howling mob, catcalls, jeering audience, booing crowd or it can be just anything or even flying tomatoes and egg shells for that matter...you can't just handle all these at first. But observe and learn from experienced speakers as to how they handle such hostile situations. Assessing audience mood, situation analysis, acting with presence of mind (remember Einstein's chauffeur?) etc will be of help in avoiding such unpleasant encounters.

If you suffer from a clear out in the middle of a speech, politely tell the audience so and go on to the next topic. Don't just stare and blink at the ceiling straining every nerve to remember your carefully prepared speech. The ensuing silence and giggles would unnerve you and shatter your confidence. Also never try to cover up such clear outs with false facts, pet theories, etc. The audience will lose credibility in the speaker and think that he is telling a bunch of lies. It's all normal to face such embarrassing clear outs midway through a speech for beginners. Only constant practice, excellent preparation and fool-proof rehearsals will help you to get over clear outs.

Handling Faux Pas and Gaffes

Faux pas and gaffes is something everyone does at one point or other. It is more pronounced when making a speech. It may be due to the psychological pressure built up within the speaker to make his speech a success. Public speakers who are on the constant move over different time zones are more prone to make faux pas and gaffes. This may be due to jet lag and exhaustion. It is normal for a speaker to make faux pas in early days and needs to be overcome only through sheer practice and rehearsal before the speech. You can't be sure how your audience may react to such faux pas though laughter is the normal response. Laugh with them and don't make yourself appear foolish by not joining them and getting annoyed. That's one nice way to face-saving. Apologise and continue with the speech. But ensure that you don't repeat them in future.

Let your Reactions be Tactful

In some cases, one among the audience may interrupt you with questions and doubts or contradict you. Let such persons be known that you would set aside some time after the speech to address the issues raised. Or simply apologise when caught quoting wrong facts. But don't forget to thank the person for setting you right. And while thanking do it with a smile and the guy would feel honored. If it is too tough extricate yourself with wit and it needs presence of mind. Just because you are on the stage you can't ramble on and on without getting pointed out. And while telling it, say with a smile without showing any show of emotions like annoyance, anger or irritation. Camouflage your emotions like anxiety or anger subtly that none can detect it at all. Simply put, be prepared for any eventuality. Don't take your audience for granted. Hope for the best but be prepared for the worst.

Be tactful while responding to questions from the audience. If someone asks questions for which you don't have the answer, honestly tell so, speak the truth but never think that you can get away with misleading or wrong answers. The audience will like and admire your frankness and forthright admission. After all it requires a sort of courage to accept your mistakes before a large number of people and very few have such guts.

Choose your Words with Care

Choose your words with care because it may hurt people for the causes they stand for. An offending remark is enough to shatter all the good will you enjoy with your audience. What good points you said will be forgotten but not that single offending remark. Know that people are very sensitive these days. Play safe. Desist from starting on an offensive note. Be a moderate in your ideas and opinions. Neither cling to extremities nor make criticisms. But make no compromises on core values. On the other hand, praise. Be lavish in your praise and everyone loves to hear it. Be aware that what you say matters as much as how you say.

Take a leaf out of a diplomat's notebook, "A diplomat is a person who can tell you to go to hell in such a way that you will really look forward to the trip".

Be clear and articulate your message in an unambiguous way. Never give room for people to misunderstand, misinterpret and misquote.

Be careful about what you say. Think twice before uttering a word. Sometime back I attended a function where the speaker was a bit annoyed with the man who came to adjust the mike. Perturbed that he was disturbing the irritated speaker said,

"Hey! You idiot! What are you doing?"

The mike man sported a perplexed look and must have wondered what on earth he made anything funny that made the entire hall to roar with laughter and this prolonged the laugh even more. Absent-mindedness doesn't go well with the audience. So be alert. A hundred pair of ears is keenly waiting for your words to pour out of your mouth.

Have patience. Patience is one important quality a speaker must develop or else it easily shows off. The impatience of a speaker is easy to notice. Bear in mind perhaps a thousand pair of eyes are watching in unison at one single individual — the speaker and realize how easy it is to spot his weaknesses.

Avoid mumbling words and fumbling for words. It shows the speaker in poor light. And avoid it even more or better still don't speak anything at all when you are pinned up with a microphone though you may be away from your audience. For a switched on microphone relays to the waiting audience whatever you speak to others.

Don't Antagonize your Audience

Never make the mistake of antagonizing your audience by saying things uncharitable and unpalatable to them lest the crowd will be on its feet making mayhem and order beyond control. None likes to be criticized. Do you?

Give, don't Expect Anything

While giving a speech always concentrate on what you can offer to the audience and not the other way around. Share your knowledge and ideas. It's one way of achieving immortality.

There are some speakers whose speeches are not colorful but they look out for applause from the listeners. Little do they realize their shortcomings. Don't expect applause in initial stages and also don't deliver speeches with the sole intent of receiving deafening applause. Have the grace and dignity to accept the situation...silence even if you are not given your due recognition and your share of applause. It means that your efforts didn't go well and you need to improve further. Applause is a genuine sign of whole-hearted appreciation given by the listeners. A good speech will automatically make the audience to give a big hand while a poor one will be greeted with catcalls, sneers and impatient thumping of desks and feet. Do your best and leave the rest to your audience. They are the right persons to judge instantly and decide whether you are worthy of bouquets or brickbats. The points you make whether they went home or not matters.

Excellent orators' speeches are punctuated frequently by audience applause and if they are really worth, it is little surprise that at the end or sometimes at the beginning of the speech they receive a thunderous standing ovation.

Remember Goethe's saying, "The deed is everything, the glory is nothing".

Tolerate Distractions

Learn to tolerate distractions for good measure for the world is full of them and the lecture hall is not an exception. It may come in different forms and be irritating. It may be intermittent coughing, a wailing child, someone in the corner seat dozing off, noise from folding plastic covers, loud music from the neighborhood or it may be as simple as ringing cell phones to an attention-distracting scene like the guy in the front row nodding his head vigorously to everything you say. You will have to develop the patience to put up with such irritants. But if it proves intolerable then kindly request to cease and desist. I repeat, make only a request not an order. Let the person who disturbs you to save his face for it feels awful to be rebuked by the speaker over the mike in front of hundreds of spectators. If you say it in a polite way, you will earn the goodwill even from the person who distracts you leave alone the audience.

Use Visual Aids

Modern technologies have enabled public speakers to achieve a great deal. For example, the mike has dispensed away the need to shout in order to be heard as in olden days. Later day innovations have miniaturized the mike so small that the speaker can just be pinned on to the dress. Cordless mikes give the speaker convenience of mobility. Using visual aids will make the speech more engaging and memorable. These include charts, graphs, pictures, etc. Today a modern speaker can use the Over Head Projector (OHP) and a Liquid Crystal Display (LCD) panel to reach out to his audience effectively. Various software applications help in making our presentations and speeches easier to get across. Power point is one such software which helps greatly in making a powerful presentation. While using technology as an aid in your speech make yourself very familiar in using it. If you are going to have someone to assist in operating the devices, get the timing right. Things have to be coordinated well. What you say and what the audiences see should go hand in hand. To play safe, rehearse well ahead with your assistant.

Modern speakers must take advantage of these latest gadgets and software and make most of the situation wherever possible. The impact of making such speeches would linger long and as such the importance of these cannot be looked over. Remember that,

"I read I can't remember
I listen I forget
I see I remember."

When you are one among the Speakers...

When you are one among a group of speakers, you can thank your stars and use the opportunity to excel others. It will be too easy to notice the performance and success of each speaker. Each one will have his own style of speech.

So resolve yourself to beat them all with your brilliant performance.

Another crucial quality people will notice is how you are attentive to other speakers. They will watch your mannerisms, attentiveness and gestures you make when another speaker booms over the mike. Many co-speakers yawn, look away or simply get busy browsing their own speeches. Don't let the same mistake to happen since it is more glaring to do all these sitting in the dais before hundreds of people. Stay as attentive as possible. Take a keen interest in what other speakers have got to say and you can give some words of praise and appreciation about them. This will show you in a different perspective and the audience will think well of you. For you had been attentive all through the other speaker's speech and not become pre-occupied with the preparations of your own speech. Also you will learn others' views and opinions.

Take Feedback

When addressing audiences familiar to you try to get feedback after the speech about your performance. Feedback will keep you focused and provide an opportunity to rectify mistakes, if any. Work upon the suggestions given. The audience is the best judge in commenting on your speech and be prepared to welcome it. It will be helpful to you.

Speak with Your Heart

Speakers who talk from their heart and not from prepared text will have more effect on the audience. People will be moved and do as you bid and see reason in your talk. While making appeals a heart-felt outpouring will make more sense and will have the desired effect.

The Finishing Touch

And while finishing a speech summarise key points for the benefit of the audience all the points — a sort of a quick recap and end with the hope or conclude it in such a way that a feel good factor prevails wishing everyone well and everyone will feel happy and glad about hearing about your speech. It not only stops there but also the audience will look forward eagerly to come to hear you again.

The Stuff is Important

All said and done, it doesn't mean that you are a straight away success in your speech. Having known and mastered the nuances of public speaking and not confident in the subject will put in a spot. The topic you choose must be familiar to you and you must feel confident in delivering the speech. Remember, my friend, many an accomplished speaker has been swept off the track due to lack of knowledge in the subject they speak. However, a skilful orator will find ways and means to escape from such traps and make his way out, somehow or other, without losing his image and the audience unaware of his discomfiture.

Be Prepared for Criticism

As with any public personality, public speakers too will be subject to criticisms which may be harsh and personal. Be ready to receive them and don't be thin skinned. Take unduly harsh criticism in your stride rather than to sulk in misery. Criticisms serve their purpose to the extent that it keeps you focused.

Introspection must follow after every round of criticism. Get into the bottom of such charges and if found really true ensure that you don't repeat them in future.

Learn but not Copy

Hear as many speeches as possible by different speakers. Closely watch their gestures, body language, postures and the like. Learn different styles of speech delivery. Learn but never copy. For it is easy to make out the imitation. Be an original and natural striving to develop a distinct style for yourself.

Constantly Improve

Improvement is one aspect which has always room. Use every public speaking opportunity to evaluate your performance and find out the causes for any lapse and take steps to constantly improve your performance. Measures for improvement are not a one-time affair. It is a continuous and on-going process.

Each public speaking engagement will not be the same from before. Every opportunity will be a unique experience from which you will have to learn and the experience thus gained must be used as a springboard for improvement.

Once you feel at ease with public speaking, incorporate higher and difficult skills that would enhance your performance. Dramatize your speech but don't over do it. For people would accuse you of over-action. Make a point animatedly so that you fire the imagination of the audience.

Become a lively Master of Ceremonies

Once you root yourself firmly as a good public speaking it is time that you venture into other areas like being the master of ceremonies.

To become one, you must have absolute confidence, proficiency and fluency in one or more languages, ready wit, enthusiasm, sharp memory, expert knowledge of many subjects and of course, presence of mind in abundance. Bear in mind, most occasions will be informal. This is a highly demanding job both physically and psychologically. So go full steam to learn the nuances and tricks of mastering this wonderful art. Being an extrovert by nature helps as also having the passion to talk and meet different people. You must be highly articulate. Inhibitions have no place in this vocation.

Get to know, in advance, of the schedule of programmes, the star performers and their profiles and conduct the event in a very lively, fun-filled and enjoyable manner. Normally people eagerly wait for the programmes but don't have the patience to listen to the announcer. It all depends on the person performing the master of ceremonies to capture and captivate the hearts of his audience and they will love to hear him as much as the events. Love your job and do your best and later you will begin enjoying your own performance. You will become indispensable in any function and be the life of the party. Soon it will be out and out your show all the way with the crowd clamoring for more.

Professionals like event managers, jockeys, commentators can be taken as good examples and closely studied for their style and performance. Attend and watch different masters of ceremonies as to how they conduct the event, react to people and handle tricky situations. Such observations will give you the idea and example to follow your own attempt.

Extempore is Possible

As you mature as a good speaker, you will develop the confidence to deliver speeches extempore. But extempore speeches need a lot of efforts on your part. Your mind needs to be alert and sharp. It needs to have very good memory and be able to handle any topic given at short notice. For this you need to be a voracious reader and have knowledge on any topic. A range of subjects must come to your mind at your beck and call. Simply put, you will have to be a "Jack of all" for the time being. Keep your eyes and ears open always. The sub-conscious mind is so powerful that even a thought which you consider as insignificant residing deep inside the mind will surface and help you at the right time. With the gaining of experience and knowledge you will almost become a walking encyclopedia. Most politicians are adept in making extempore speeches that the teeming millions are won over instantly by their erudition and mastery of their subject.

Mastery in extempore will come only with the passage of time by the experience you gain. It is a long haul spread over a number of years. In an extempore speech, psychological pressure will be more than in a well-prepared speech and hence the chances for committing faux pas and gaffes are more. To avoid getting into awkward positions first speak not all you think. Structure your thoughts and speak cautiously. Thought and speech coordination reigns supreme in an extempore performance.

A word of caution. Never attempt extempore in the initial stages even though the audience is familiar to you. It will be a disastrous one and put you off.

Speaking extempore is another kind of public speaking and very few have mastered it and achieved immense success in it. And those few always enjoy the awe and wonder of their audiences.

Build your Image

Do your best since you are carving an image for yourself and be careful about building it and maintaining it. Speak to inform and inspire but not to display your erudition. Tell things that are positive and highlight good aspects as opposed to negative feelings and I am sure it will have an impact on the listeners.

The exact words you spoke may be forgotten after some time. The message, if inspiring and worthy will linger for long. Even with the passage of time people may forget the message. But they will remember you if your performance is par excellence. It's just like customers forgetting the price but not the quality!

Image is like reputation: difficult to earn, easy to lose and extremely hard to regain.

Endspeak

With good public speaking skills you are, on your own right, on your way to become from obscurity to celebrity!

Just by reading this book you cannot expect yourself to gain mastery over public speaking. No amount of bookish knowledge will suffice. Only through practice and keen observation you can learn this art. Or else it will be like learning to swim without getting anywhere near water. You must avail all opportunities that present before you and make most of it. Mind you, opportunity is not the one to regularly knock your door.

If you had noticed, one quality which all public speakers present is a picture of confidence. They are never afraid of anything. Fearlessness is one quality you will find in them. With the language command and erudition they can do what they want with their audience.

Once you are adept in public speaking, people will sit spell bound for hours together as if in trance waiting hungrily for each word to flow out like honey. After a successful lecture you will feel that everyone hung on your lips!

There are only uninteresting speakers but not uninteresting subjects. Even a dry subject will become interesting if you listen to expert public speakers. For instance, whenever the late legal luminary, Nani A. Palkhivala spoke, people used to flock to hear him in droves. The venue — a football stadium will overflow with people, from the layman to professionals to hear him speak on topics supposed to be dry and uninteresting like taxation and law!

Public speakers are as popular as pop stars. The difference being the type of audience by whom they are sought out. The former is liked by knowledge-seekers and the latter by fun-loving masses.

All said but don't expect to learn the art of public speaking from a mere book. This is only theory; observation and rehearsals are practice. With the mastery of this skill you can start winning and get noticed among the top echelons of your organization. You will become famous and find yourself in the limelight just because you are a good speaker.

Didn't you feel awful and jealous when a smart kid in your class dominated it with mere fluency in English? And now imagine what power you hold when you can cast your charm over a large number of people with the art of public speaking!

Presentation Skills

What you say is as important as how you say.

Presentation skill is one aspect which many professionals in their early part of their career fail to master. It is very crucial for putting forth what you have got to say in a very effective manner.

Presentation skill is important whether you are seeking to put forward your ideas and thoughts, views and opinions through a speech or through writing. These skills help you to present your thoughts in a structured manner instead of a haphazard and cluttered way. However, here we are discussing only about verbal presentation.

Simply put, presentation skill involves putting forth "Maximum facts in Minimum time" in such a way that it is more meaningful and easy to comprehend for the target audience.

Presentation skills are necessary:

- To present your thoughts in a structured manner instead of a haphazard and cluttered way.
- To make comprehension easy for others as to what you intend to say.

- To explain tough concepts and ideas in a simple manner.
- To say what you want when time is limited.
- To describe in brief of what would normally be lengthy.

Presentation skill makes your job easier and simple. Brevity is the hallmark in using this skill. And at the same time this brevity doesn't cost the clarity that goes with any communication.

You well know what to say but more often than not how to say. This anomaly is effectively addressed by the mastery of presentation skills. Very few would have the patience and time to sit through a lengthy and boring speech and here is where presentation skills come to the rescue of the speaker. When put to right use people would not only be informed adequately within the limited time but also be appreciative of your efforts.

Presentation skills, now-a-days, has been used effectively with unknown but powerful audience. Take for instance the case of modern and progressive Chief Ministers using their presentation skills to the hilt to inform, impress and intimidate top officials from the World Bank and other cash-rich entities to part with whopping sums of money!

Or for that matter you can learn from lawyers. For lawyers without adequate presentation skills wouldn't fare better. See how meticulous they will have to work in constructing their arguments based on facts and evidences and present their case before the judge or a panel of jurists and win for their clients.

Present your case to achieve what you want. To make this possible you will have to possess the power of persuasion, salesmanship, clarity of expression and thought.

For every professional it is imperative to learn this skill. Be it the marketing man, accountant or engineer or the software professional every one will at one point of time or other will have to make a presentation before their superiors. The sales rep will have to make a presentation as to the sales plan for the next, say, 2 years or so, the accountant has to explain the fund requirements and budget for the coming months, the engineer has to present his product design and technical specifications for approval and the software techie has to describe his project details, etc.

The main objectives in presenting is to put things forward in a very clear way structuring your points in some sequence, logically constructed, proceeding to higher concepts in a graded manner that is easy to follow for your audience. In simple terms, presentation skills aim to put complex concepts in a simple manner.

Since all busy professionals are hard pressed for time, presentation skills will help them to get across their message correctly.

The Basics

People who are good public speakers mostly are adept in presenting their message. As for them to learn presentation skills either the necessity doesn't arise or need only a small orientation on their part just to get things right.

Unlike the public speaker, the person who is going to make presentation has the edge since he is more informed and knows his audience well in most cases. This element of familiarity with the audience is more crucial to his success.

Other than these, the presenter must, more or less, have most of the skills that make a good public speaker. These include amongst other things, making eye-contact, employing appropriate gestures and body language and voice modulation. Also ensure that you don't lose track of the time and preferably make your presentation short. Remember "First impression is best impression". Your presentation must be convincing, persuasive and aim to fulfill the objectives with which you set out in your endeavor.

The Spadework

Before presenting yourself plan well ahead as to the following aspects:

- What topic you need to present?
- Who is your target audience?
- Whether you need to give handouts?

- How long is your presentation going to be?
- Whether OHP/LCD facilities are available? If available, the necessary preparations to use them during your presentation.

When you are in spotlight it is easy to say the wrong thing. This reflects not only your caliber but also your company. The difference between winning and losing can hinge on the impression you make. For top performance (to get the desired results), people need to be top communicators.

Interact to Interest

Tell me and I'll forget; show me and I may remember; involve me and I'll understand.

—Chinese proverb

A good presenter wouldn't dare to make his presentation session a one-way communication. Rather he would prefer to make it interactive by throwing questions or inviting them from his audience so that he can be doubly sure that everyone is listening and the message has gone down. Such interactions would hold audience interest and make it mutually beneficial both to the presenter and the audience.

Technology Aids Presentation

Today's technology helps the modern executive to present with an impact. Verbal presentation is complemented well by taking advantage of the latest devices and gadgets. Contemporary presentations are never complete without visual aids.

In order to effectively drive home your message, you must learn to use modern devices and gadgets. Familiarity with Over Head Projectors (OHP), Liquid Crystal Device (LCD) panel and proficiency in one or two presentation software will be of immense help.

Presentation software like MS-Power Point aids greatly in making a powerful presentation. What you say when it is told with visual aids makes a tremendous impression among the audience.

Normally, you would be using slides to present your ideas and concepts. Learn to prepare them on your own since you would be able to appreciate the working of them better. Slides which are the objects of attention must be very attractive to the beholders. Never use paragraphs. Put the concept in points either numbering or bulleting them. Also ensure that the font is large enough so that even the guys at the last row can see clearly.

While using technology as an aid in your speech make yourself very familiar in using it. If you are going to have someone to assist in operating the devices, get the timing right. Things have to be coordinated well to avoid embarrassing goof-ups while doing the presentation. What you say and what the audiences see should go hand in hand. To play safe, rehearse well ahead with your assistant.

The chief advantages in using digital presentation are to make your performance more effective, engaging and memorable one.

Hand Outs

Handouts are necessary since they summarise the points you speak. They need to be given to the audience so that they will act upon it in future. What is the fun in simply speaking and going away? What you say, at least some part of it must stay in people's minds and not get carried away with the air. When there are a number of speakers what you said may be quickly forgotten. There needs to be some impact and people need to refer to your speech at a later point of time. Handouts help in serving this purpose.

Handouts must be very brief and upto the point. But it must also cover all the points at least the important ones. Diagrams, charts and other visual aids can be used. Don't use lengthy paragraphs as none will have the time and patience to read through them. Break the concepts into points. Number them or use bullets. Economy is the watchword in handout preparation. A glance over the handout must be able to drive home the message. In short, they need to be crisp and short. That is where the power of handout lies. Also see that handouts don't exceed more than two papers.

Be sure that everyone in the audience is provided with a copy of handout as being left out will unnecessarily make people go red. So ascertain the exact number of people attending your presentation and have extra copies of the same in good measure. For you can't be sure of how many turning up.

Ensure that you give handouts after your presentation and never before. For giving prior would steal the sheen away and people would know what you have got to say and subsequently lose interest. Also there is every chance that people will tend to read rather than pay attention to you.

Time is Precious

Presentations are usually of short duration. And it all depends how much of the points you are going to cover effectively within this short time.

While preparing for presentations ensure that you cover all the necessary points well within the allotted time. Make it a well-structured one. To ensure this you will have to rehearse at least a couple of times. Ascertain the duration of your presentation and prepare accordingly.

Be conscious of the time all through. Glance your watch discreetly so that you keep track of the time. Never try to carry on after your allotted time since that is not a sign of good preparation. Also others may be waiting and none can sit through your presentation for long. But oblige and continue only if asked to do so. If your presentation is lengthy and full of tough facts to digest, give people a short break. While doing so say "Lets get back by 11.00 am" instead of saying "Lets have a 5-minute break". Be specific in your instructions.

Attire and Appearance

The attire, no doubt, is formal wear. Formal wear gives a professional look to your image. Be impeccably dressed. Since you would be making the presentation in a small conference hall (as opposed to auditoriums) with your audience it will be easy to look at you in close quarters. Make sure that your dress is pressed well and shoes are polished well. Belts must have the gloss to avoid eyesores. Using a hanky will save you from embarrassment but don't hold it all through the presentation. A good pen in your shirt pocket completes your image.

Your appearance counts a lot since people will observe you closely. Do all you can to appear as a well-groomed person. Avoid using strong perfumes as it may put people off due to its overbearing fragrance spreading all over the room.

Perform your Best

Research thoroughly your topic and do your home work well. You must be prepared for facing any questions and clearing doubts and clarifications. Since the audience in most cases will be familiar to you, some degree of informality can be expected. Questions may fly at the drop of hat and you must know how to handle them. Train up your memory so that you can get back to where you left after such interruptions.

Usually you will be allotted with some time after your presentation to take questions from the audience. Put up a brave face and answer sincerely and truthfully. If you don't have the right answers say so and assure that you will get back to them later. Don't try to mislead or give wrong answers as it will terribly affect your credibility.

Endspeak

Most qualities and skills that make a good public speaker are fully applicable to make your presentation a success. In other words, a good presenter basically should have good public speaking abilities.

Having mastered presentation skills you can count yourself as a good communicator since all good presenters are articulate in voicing their thoughts and ideas. With good presentation skills you can even get jobs, win over your superiors and get a new image among the top echelons of your organisation. People will begin to take notice of you solely because of this wonderful skill and this is something that cannot be easily overlooked away.

Good presentation skills will fetch you important assignments and propel you to the top long before you expect that to happen. So see that you employ the best of your talents and communication skills in making a power-packed presentation and you are well on the way to success.

Technology Aids Communication

Science and technology multiply around us. To an increasing extent they dictate the languages in which we speak and think. Either we use those languages, or we remain mute.

—J.G. Ballard

Today's technology that is available to the busy executive is really astounding in its range and sweep. Without the usage of these modern conveniences communication will be slow and human progress wouldn't have been possible.

Some of the common and widely used modes of communication in the corporate world are listed out.

1. Telephone

The telephone has proved to be a great way to communicate, save time, energy and resources. All we need to do is to simply dial a number and get the person on the line and talk. People are just a call away. It is a convenient way to get to talking with people any where in the world. Today we just can't imagine an office without a telephone.

2. Pager

Not bigger than your wallet, a pager is a handy piece of electronic device which helps others to communicate with you. It is very useful when you are on the move. You could get the latest updates of news, advertisements and games too. Ensure that you keep your pager switched on always.

3. E-mail

Electronic mail or e-mail is the most popular of all written communication modes since it is fast, reliable and simple to use. With the advent of internet, e-mail has changed the way we communicate with each other. Inter-office memos have become extinct and email has ushered in the 'paper-less' office concept. E-mail is very flexible since it allows us to send messages with attachments to any number of persons and mark copies to as many as people as we want. Forwarding the same message is another convenient way to communicate.

E-mail's convenience, rapidity and efficiency has made people to dub postal services as 'snail mail'. Whether it rains or shines, postal strike or trucker's strike, it doesn't matter. It is common nowadays to see employees have allotted corporate e-mail ID by the organizations they work for.

Corporate communications has undergone a sea-change with the emergence of e-mail. Communication is smooth, fast and secure. Above all, it keeps everyone in the loop.

4. Internet

Perhaps the most revolutionary innovation of human genius is the internet. It is a grand network of networks of computers connected globally. Even if a person spends his whole life-time in surfing the net for information he cannot complete the task. For the information available in the cyberspace is staggering and colossal. Information of any subject under the sun is available and people can gain a lot from using this powerful medium by downloading the necessary quantum. Progressive companies have their own websites through which they disseminate information about their mission, objectives, activities, products and services, etc.

5. Chatting

Chatting though mostly used in informal communication has been gaining ground as a powerful and effective way to communicate in the corporate world. People can contact others in any place and start exchanging view points by typing through the internet-enabled personal computer. For this to happen, two or more people should be logged in at the same time through computers in a virtual place called chatroom. More people can join subsequently without hindering the on-going communication and participate in the discussion. Reply comes immediately on the screen and this kind of communication can be compared to be the written equivalent of wireless exchanges. Your response needs to be quick and crisp. Given the constraints of time, lengthy messages make it boring to read and understand. So do your homework well before starting a chatting session.

6. Cellular Phone

Cellular phone shortened to cell phone or simply cell these days are the most common form of communication. It is just a telephone miniaturized to the size of your wallet without the usual frills — the wires. They are handy and can be carried along anywhere we go — its mobile and thus the other name — mobile phone. Short messaging service (SMS) is a new innovation in cell phone where brief communication can be sent.

Thought there are arguments against the usage of cell phones on health point of view, nothing substantial has been proved so far so as to confirm the apprehensions raised by alarmists.

7. Video Conferencing

Organising and conducting meetings can be expensive when the participants have to come from distant geographic locations and spending huge sums of money for travel and stay. Video conferencing is the solution as it helps to overcome constraints imposed by time, geographic distances and it dispenses away with the need to travel. Meetings through video conferencing are possible when PCs are attached with small cameras and excellent hi-speed telecommunication lines are available. It not only saves money but also ensures a speedier review and feedback system.

8. Fax

Facsimile transmission or simply fax is communication device that helps in sending messages just as we want to appear. For example, you can fax a letter or note for approval to the receiver in your own letter-head. The receiver will have to print your communication. The communication is instant and as such it saves time. To communicate via fax, you need to have access to fax machine and know the receiver's fax number just like the telephone number. Type/write out the message in a neat sheet of paper, insert into the fax machine and dial the number. If the machine at the other end is free it will receive your message.

9. Internet Telephony

Internet Telephony is one of the latest communication technologies which is in nascent stages in some countries. Popularly known as net-2-phone, internet telephony blends telephone and internet for communications. One can chat through this medium at expenses which are normally lower than ISD calls.

10. Software in PC — Winpop and Power Point

Winpop from Microsoft is a wonderful facility to communicate messages in an informal setting. Short messages can be sent over a network of computers to the recipient. The message flashes over the computer screen. It will be fun to use this software.

Presentation graphics software complements our efforts while making presentations. Microsoft's Power Point is popular software which helps us to graphically present in a very clear and concise way. Learning to use this software will be very useful for presenters.

11. LCD/OHP

Liquid Crystal Display (LCD) is used to display images, text and video to viewers. The output is excellent due to the clarity LCDs offer. During presentations the presentation graphic software is projected through a LCD panel. It does the job of a PC monitor except that the screen is big enabling viewers to see from distance clearly.

Over-Head Projectors (OHP) is less expensive when compared to LCD panels. Though it does the same job of a LCD, instead of projecting through a PC a projector is used. Transparencies must be prepared and placed inside the OHP machine to project the contents on to the screen.

12. Mike

Mike, the ubiquitous of all, needs no introduction since it is the most common of all modes of communication. When the audience is huge and the speaker wants to make himself heard a mike comes handy. Innovations have miniaturized the size of mikes and today mikes can be pinned up on the shirt and it can be held by hand sans wires.

With the bewildering array of modern communication mediums the means of personal contact has decreased. Communication through technology only helps us to mitigate the constraints imposed by time, travel and distance. But one fact remains to be borne in mind. Whatever mode of technology it may be, or however convenient it may be to use there is nothing equal to the communication which it is direct, carried on in person, face-to-face.

Real communication takes place when one human being reaches out to other by using his natural modes of communication supplemented by personal charisma. Remember that all the audio/visual/multimedia in the world cannot replace the charm and power of the human voice with all its personal charisma, body language with appropriate emotions. Yet use technology to make communication easier, simpler, faster and effective.

The Seven Cs of Effective Communication

1. Completeness

- Provide all necessary information.
- Answer all questions asked.
- Give something extra, when desirable.
- Answer the 5 Ws — What, When, Where, Why and Who.

2. Conciseness

- Eliminate wordy expressions.
- Include only relevant material.
- Avoid unnecessary repetition.

3. Consideration

- Focus on 'You' instead of 'I' or 'We'.
- Show audience benefit or interest in the receiver.
- Emphasise positive, pleasant facts.

4. Concreteness

- List out specific facts and figures.
- Put action in your verbs.
- Choose vivid, image building words.

5. Clarity

- Employ precise, concrete and familiar words.
- Construct effective sentences and paragraphs.
- Build coherent paragraphs.

6. Courtesy

- Be sincerely tactful, thoughtful and appreciative.
- Use expressions that show respect.
- Choose non-discriminating expression.

7. Correctness

- Use the right level of language.
- Stick to facts and check the accuracy of figures, facts and words.
- Maintain acceptable writing style.

4

BUSINESS ETIQUETTE AND PERSONAL GROOMING

The Mark of a Gentleman

- Seven Ways to be the Perfect Gentleman
  - (1) Sport the Professional Look
  - (2) Addressing People
  - (3) Managing Emotions
  - (4) Table Manners
  - (5) How to be an Official Diplomat?
  - (6) Treating Visitors
  - (7) The Art of Conversation
- Technology Etiquette

Business etiquette and personal grooming are important for today's executive to excel and shine in his career. These are not the ends in itself perhaps the means to promote yourself as a well-groomed person who knows what is what and knows how to go about doing his job.

Schools and colleges help you to gain degrees and doctorates, but seldom focus on good manners and behavior. Many professionals despite high academic achievements and top qualifications have turned out to be big failures when it comes to business etiquette. In order to address this anomaly, it is imperative that you take your first steps to learn business etiquette and personal grooming. It helps in more than one way.

Learning business etiquette and personal grooming helps you in the following ways:

1. You sport a well-cultured and well-mannered image.

2. You don't feel at sea when exposed to people who are superior to you. You are at ease as a socialite or in a social setting.
3. You learn how to react and behave in different situations.
4. They give you self-respect and confidence.
5. It reflects your class and projects you as a person of high caliber.

In learning business etiquette the ground rules are few:

1. Remember, just like oil and water, booze, drugs and business don't mix.
2. Never take anybody for granted.
3. Handle people with care. Everyone — subordinate, peer and superior should be treated with equal courtesy and respect. Simply, it would mean treating all as you would wish to be treated yourself.

Business etiquette means give and take, helping each other when help is needed or sought and being considerate of others. Mind you, here we are not talking about social etiquette since it has its own set of rules.

People begin observing you when your behavior and mannerisms show how cultured and groomed you are. You will be able to integrate better, socialize and feel at home with business etiquette. You will find yourself loved by everyone, invited everywhere and be seen with top notch people.

Haven't you seen people like those in the hospitality business? The poise, charm and grace in conducting business — all customer-centric. Achieving job excellence with their personal charisma and personality with good manners and behavior and in the course of the task earning the good will of the people they are dealing with. Yet it wouldn't be possible to get things done and receive plaudits except for one wonderful soft skill — business etiquette and personal grooming!

Seven Ways to be the Perfect Gentleman

The king can make a knight, but not a gentleman

Learning business etiquette and personal grooming leads a person to take the first step towards becoming the perfect gentleman. In the process, you strive yourself to project you in your best behavior and grace. Gentlemen have gentle manners. But it doesn't mean that you will have to be pushed over by others. It's all about being gentle but firm, assertive instead of aggressive and courteous but not cowing down.

A gentleman is not the one who smokes Hedges & Benson, donning a Reid and Taylor suit, Rolex watch, arriving by chauffeur driven Mercedes, playing cricket and golf. In fact, personality and lifestyle alone don't make a perfect gentleman. It is his behavior and attitude towards others and the deeds he performs that counts.

To enunciate further I narrate a story told by Sister Nivedita. Once when she was giving a send-off to Jagdish Chandra Bose, the great scientist of India and his family at the Calcutta Railway Station the carriages were full and jam-packed. Somehow they found a carriage which was bare except for a couple of Englishmen who were sitting inside. Hardly had they tried to board when the Englishmen shouted at them and locked the doors. All protests were in vain. Their only sin was that they were Indians and as such they cannot travel with English 'gentlemen'. Luckily, they found room in another carriage where a villager was sitting across the seats. The latter who was smoking hookah as soon as he saw the ladies occupying the seats stopped smoking, put away the hookah and gave room for the family. Sister Nivedita, herself an Englishwoman who dedicated her life for the cause of betterment of India, compared and praised the gentlemanly behavior of the 'uncultured' villager with that of the 'cultured' Englishmen.

Another incident which is well-known and you must be knowing. When Mahatma Gandhi went to London for the Round Table Conference in 1931, he was granted an audience with His Majesty the King of England. Horrified by his 'uncultured' attire of a dhoti and shawl, the Mahatma was advised to dress like Englishmen before he presents himself to the King. To which he answered that he would definitely not ask the King to dress like him if he was to be invited! Should I say more? He met the King just as it is.

The point here is clothes alone don't make a gentleman. There is more to meet the eye before you say someone as a gentleman.

As such, among other things I believe, the following seven topics will help a person in his efforts to become the perfect gentleman:

1. Sport a professional look
2. Addressing People
3. Managing Emotions
4. Table Manners
5. How to be an Official Diplomat?
6. Treating Visitors
7. The Art of Conversation

No doubt, learning and adopting these are sure signs of a perfect gentleman!

SPORT THE PROFESSIONAL LOOK

Dress like a gentleman and you act like a gentleman.
Clothes create an impression you must live upto.

Time and again, you have been wondering what does this phrase "Sport a professional look" really means. It's all about presenting yourself as a well-groomed person and appearing business-like. For this to happen, you needn't have to be necessarily handsome or beautiful, just clean and neat. Your external personality is the first thing that people notice and many tend to judge people by appearances alone. Of course, looks too matter since they are the ones that help in creating that first impression and it must be the best.

First Impressions Matter Most

We all know that first impressions are best impressions and perhaps lasting ones. Take meticulous care of the impression you create whenever you meet someone, present yourself for an interview, handover your business card or resume, write or reply to someone, speak over the telephone

— all for the first time. Remember, you will never, never have a second chance to create an impression on others. So get it right the first time.

Appearance

Appearance matters a lot in business. Our appearance shapes how others perceive us at first look and later. Let's start with the basics. A well-groomed personality will

1. Clean teeth daily twice.
2. Bath or shower daily.
3. Use deodorant and mouthwash.
4. Keep his hair cut and trimmed once in every 4 weeks or so.
5. Manicure nails and keep it clean.
6. Wear only stain-free clothes that are laundered, pressed and dry cleaned.
7. Replace old and frayed watch straps.
8. Keep shoes and belts polished and shiny. Wear only executive length socks.
9. Use only good quality perfume, cologne and after-shave but ensures that it is mild and not over bearing.
10. Use handkerchiefs not tissue papers.

Attire

Clothes maketh a man.

Attire is important since it reflects your personality. As a general rule, wear clothes with which you feel comfortable. Your attire should be of good quality and reflect you and your company's image. Whether you wear clothes according to your choice or company uniform some decorum needs to be followed. Some guidelines are listed below:

1. Invest in good quality business suits. Wear clothes for you and not for others.
2. Learn to fix your tie properly.
3. Creaseless and dirt-free attire is a must.
4. Wear colors which are not gaudy and flashy.
5. Clothes which are torn, shrunk and faded are a strict no-no.

6. Try out before you buy. Suitability alone is not the consideration.
7. Don't get carried away by latest design craze and fashions.
8. Wear dresses befitting the occasion. Tuck in always.
9. Informal wear may be appropriate while traveling and informal parties.
10. A neat business-looking pen must complete your attire.

If your job entails you to sit late on a daily basis, keep a pair of clean socks and a good shirt at your office. With them you may perform better. To deal with emergencies have a sewing kit handy. Remember to dress better than your clients but not that of your boss.

Countenance

Continual cheerfulness is a sign of wisdom.

—Irish proverb

Your attire and appearance alone are not enough to complete the professional look. Your countenance matters as much as your attire. A pleasing countenance is essential. A pleasing countenance is characterized by sporting a smile and cheerful disposition. Your personality must exude confidence. As the face is the index of mind, people will easily find out what's inside you. Don't give them a chance. Positive thoughts help you to radiate positive feelings towards others. Your optimism will speak for itself through your behavior and poise. Be cheerful.

Smile!

A smile is the light in your window that tells others that there is a caring, sharing person inside.

—Denis Waitley

Above all, remember that the most beautiful attire is SMILE! Your look is never complete without it. Want a face-lift? Wear a smile. A smile helps you to create the rapport between yourself and the person you meet. It puts the other person at ease.

Your smile speaks for you even before you begin to talk. It says "I am fine. I look forward meeting you". It reflects your cheerfulness and positive thoughts. Smile supplements your positive radiance. Optimists smile. Pessimists frown. It is as simple as that. Also remember that it takes 26 muscles to smile, but 62 muscles to frown! So communicate cheerfulness and exude confidence with a beautiful smile. A smile is a simple gesture but with immense rewards. Remember Phyllis Diller's words, "A smile is a curve that sets everything straight".

SHARE A SMILE

When you're walking down the street,
Share a smile with those you meet.
If you happen to be wearing a frown,
It makes their smile turn up-side down.

Ever notice, a smile has a way
Of saying, "Hello, and have a nice day?"
Smile for a while. Don't be lonesome or blue.
Smiles are contagious! So, share one or two.

What if we all walked around looking sad?
Would we feel better, or would we feel bad?
When you give everyone around you a smile,
It makes them feel happy, at least for a while.

It's so easy to put a smile on your face.
Smiles take little time and they don't take up space.
And, a smile seems to go a very long way.
So, instead of a frown, share a smile everyday.

—Vicke Lambdin

Indeed, sport a smile every moment! Just keep smiling!

And finally remember that,

Of all the things you wear, your expression is the most important.

—Janet Lane

Our appearance attracts the spotlight since it influences how others perceive us. People judge based on their perceptions already formed about us. People start making judgments about our professionalism, social class and caliber. It's no wonder, what they see, they believe.

With a well-groomed personality you must be able to make that sort of statement which means business, at the first appearance. Now put in your best appearance and as you sport that professional look you have one external but important aspect that makes the perfect gentleman!

ADDRESSING PEOPLE

The sweetest sound next to a man's name is his title. So get it right or people may get you wrong.

Addressing people is important since people are emotional beings who may not take kindly to any faux pas or blunders. People value their qualifications and titles and they expect a degree of respect from others.

- While addressing people prefix Mr or Mrs or Ms as the case may be. Address people by their name along with appropriate titles they may have. Ex Dr, Prof, Military titles, etc.
- Every time you speak to them start with Sir or Madam. It personalizes your conversation, shows that you are aware of their presence and give due respect to them.
- Never start calling people by their first names until you are permitted to.
- When among people who are intimate to you, learn to address people by their names since for everyone his own name is the sweetest word in any language. They love, cherish, and appreciate it.
- In business correspondence, make sure that you suffix qualifications and prefix titles. Ex H.E or Hon. Raymond Smith, Prof. Bill Richardson, Ph.D
- Also use their designations properly. Don't get them wrong.

Introductions

Introductions are the first gestures in getting to know about people and even forming great friendships.

- While being introduced make eye-contact and say, "Hello" or "Glad to meet you". Simultaneously smile and extend your hand for a gentle but firm handshake.
- Prefix Mr or Ms or Dr or Prof to the name in formal situations or in deference to age or position.

- If none is there to introduce you, introduce yourself with confidence.
- If you aren't recognized, never ask "Remember me?" Re-introduce yourself.
- The younger person is introduced to the older person.
- Introduce the junior person to senior in business pecking order.
- When two people are of equal status, introduce the one you know less well to the one you know better.
- Keep introductions short. It should not be more than a couple of minutes.
- If you have problem with catching the name, ask the person to repeat. Never try to assume.

Whether you introduce people or you are being introduced sport a cheerful disposition and show interest and enthusiasm.

Business Cards

You may be wondering whether we need a discussion at all at first, about what seems to be a trivial accessory called business card. Yet the size doesn't matter but the look and feel and the way in which you handle it matters a lot.

- Business cards must have a neat layout and provide the necessary information. They must be up-to-date and printed on good quality card. If you are concerned about the eco-hazards of plastic cards, use bio-degradable plastic cards.
- Follow your company policy while putting your residential address and phone no. on the business card.
- Do not force your card on anyone or offer it early in conversation.
- Never make calls without your business card. It serves as an identity as to who you are and what you are.
- Stock them in your wallet and keep three of them separately to use them in case you run out of them.
- While forwarding a note or resume, attach your business card.

- When calling new people for the first time, send in your card first. It is good manners as it helps them to know who you are before meeting you face to face.
- Make your card look professional. No flimsy designs and color shadings.
- Suffixing your qualification is up to you. But in these modern times, people aren't concerned about crowing their own academic achievements.
- Asking for a business card shows that you are sincere about wanting to remember the person.
- Avoid correcting information with your pen and eventually spoiling the look of a business card. If the details become out-dated, abandon and replace fast. Monetarily, it matters nothing but socially it matters a lot.
- Your business card must be of the appropriate size easy to fit inside any wallet.
- When traveling abroad where the language is not English, get a set of cards printed in the local language on the other side of your card. Ensure the accuracy before distributing. This gesture will be greatly appreciated by people.
- Don't use business cards as paper notes or use it as bookmarks.
- If you lose someone's card, don't hesitate to ask one in your next meeting.
- Receive business cards with care and remember to put them separately lest you would find yourself giving others' card. Shift them to a business card album.
- Don't give your business card at a social setting unless asked for.
- When you want to distribute your business card to a group of people, place a set of them on a table. Don't pass on by hand to everyone.
- For convenience carry your business cards in a separate card holder since they wouldn't get soiled or folded.

It is said that by looking at a business card you can find out a lot about a person, his background and caliber. So get it right while addressing and introducing people fishing out your business card at the appropriate time and you can be sure that you are made up of the stuff that make a perfect gentleman!

MANAGING EMOTIONS

Life is too short for mean anxieties

—Charles Kingsley

Today's workplaces are very demanding. Just as how your Intelligence Quotient (IQ) fetched you the job your Emotional Quotient (EQ) is crucial to get along with people. We are what but slaves of emotions. We go through a kaleidoscope of emotions in our daily lives. Emotions are powerful and they dictate our behavior with others. A gentleman would always know how to manage his emotions. Maintaining one's emotional balance is vital while dealing with people.

Take a hard look at the most common negative emotions and be on guard.

Jealousy

Inadequacies and insecurities fuel jealousy

Jealousy is one emotion which easily rears up its ugly head when we see someone doing well. It could be anything from having better car to getting accolades for a job well done. It springs from our own complexes and perceptions we have about people. When we find someone 'inferior' to us overtaking us either in possessions or positions we get jealous. On the other hand, it comes from our own inabilities, shortcomings. The mind refuses to see reason and the only thought is the other person doesn't 'deserve' it.

A mind that is free from jealousy is important in life — for peace of mind. It shows the maturity of the mind to take things in its stride and carry on. It needs a big heart to extend our hand in congratulations. Jealousy has its by-products. Out of jealousy come fear, hatred and anger. Fear — because we are unable to do anything when people overtake us, hatred — because we cannot accept or digest the fact that the other guy deserves since he has done something better, anger — because we hate accepting reality — the superiority of other guy. Little wonder, the favorite pastime of jealous people is complaining.

We can be at peace with ourselves if we are not perturbed by jealousy.

Hate

I will permit no man to narrow and degrade my soul by making me hate him.

—Booker T. Washington

Hatred is very bad as it eats us from within. We lose our peace of mind when we are engulfed in hatred. Dislike in its extremity becomes hatred. The reasons are varied and many. Not long is the road from fear to hatred. When we see someone doing well we get afraid that he may supersede us. From this fear comes hatred. The object of hatred, if he is above us we don't whole-heartedly co-operate or if he works for us we get rude. Remember, rudeness is a weak man's imitation of strength.

The best antidote to hatred is the opposite — love. As you start loving people hatred vanishes.

Greed

Grasp all; lose all

Greed is nothing but the mentality to have it all, more and more. Avarice is in abundance where greed is present. Greed is the opposite of contentment. This quality is found in children who want an entire box of candies when one or two would suffice. This aggravates further when kids grow up. The greed for candies graduates into the avarice for money — tons of it. Or on the other hand, people become gluttons.

Greedy people become misers and all misers are unpopular. We all know the story of how a greedy person not content with one golden egg a day killed the goose to get all the golden eggs from its stomach. Greedy people come to a naught sooner or later. Naturally, greedy people are selfish.

I know of one guy who orders many items of the menu at a restaurant. Little he would realize he cannot eat everything by himself. What four people could eat he would order. No sooner had he eaten his second dish than he would feel enough is enough. It is a waste of money and food. For a greedy person the world is not enough!

Suspicion

Suspicion is a weed that keeps growing big and bigger

Suspicion — this is most common of bosses. This is due to their refusal to believe in people. Or due to one bitter experience. People would jump in to conclusions that a person is not fit for the job and unreliable. Some are born exclusively to suspect others — doubting Thomases.

Where there is no trust, there is suspicion. Trust is essential to get things done. If you want to be trusted, first you must trust people. Being suspicious of bad people will help detecting frauds and cover ups. But when the same is applied to good people they lose initiative and sport a resigned attitude.

Fear

Fear has magnifying eyes

Fear is the oldest and strongest emotion of mankind. Fear is nothing but weakness of the mind. This is a hangover from our childhood. We were afraid of dark as kids. Now we are afraid of people above us. Power, authority and position instill fear in us. Fear of the stick — punishment if we don't do well in our jobs dictates our behavior and actions. Fear of the unknown like death, various phobias, and unpredictability like future can be debilitating. Fear of the risks involved kills initiatives and enterprise. Fear stems from insecurities and inabilities. Magnifying problems, exaggerations are also causes of fear. There is more to lose with fear. A person with fear will die hundred times a day. The absence of courage is fear but the same cannot be said vice versa. When all your attempts to overcome fear are futile there is one more way: Keep up appearances and put up a brave face. Over a period of time, you get accustomed and fear goes away.

One remedy for overcoming fear is to doing the thing the fear, and fear will disappear. And that needs courage. "Courage is resistance to fear, mastery of fear, not the absence of fear" said Mark Twain. Beat away fear with courage. Be brave-hearted.

Arrogance

Affluence breeds arrogance

Arrogance stems from possessions — knowledge, material things, lineage, position or whatever we are proud of but others lack it. Feeling superior about oneself brings arrogance. Being adamant and stubborn is closely associated with arrogance.

Bloated egos form the basis of arrogance. Our ego exhibits its ugly side through arrogance, boastfulness and haughtiness. Arrogant people don't go far. They are bound to stumble on their way. Adamant, stubborn and obstinacy are associated with an arrogant person.

Arrogance can be explained with a short story.

It so happened that a frog found Re. 1 in its hole. Daily on their way to bath an elephant herd used to pass by the frog's hole. Whenever they were on the move the hole shook and the frog got agitated and worried about its very existence. So the next day when the elephants came the frog shouted from his hole to a tall pachyderm. "O Jumbo! If you ever pass this way again wait and see what I am going to do" little realizing that all it takes for the elephant is to put a gentle step to crush the frog to death.

Such is the predicament of man when he comes across something to possess. Arrogance takes over.

Anger

Anger is a short madness

This is one emotion we always seem to be struggling with. None of us can deny feeling it. All of us have difficulty with expressing it. Read on for suggestions on how to handle anger more effectively.

Anger is a short madness. It is a highly concentrated state of mind — negativity. It's the black sheep of emotions, we have all felt it — heart pounding, temple throbbing, fist-clenching anger. Anger if not controlled will have serious consequences on our health. Anger can't really make your blood boil, but it sure can give you a heart attack or even paralyse you. Anger comes in many shapes and forms.

Frustration: "I just can't do it; I hate it and I'll never be good at it"

Hurt: "How could you say that to me? I thought we were friends..."

Annoyance: "This is the fourth time you've been late this week..."

Disappointment: "I had everything planned for today's picnic and now it's raining".

Harassment: "I want complete silence".

Threats: "Wait and see. What I am going to do..."

Tragedy, illness: "Why me?", "It's so unfair" syndrome.

Controlling anger is the biggest challenge for us. Anger makes man a beast.

Anger is a valuable resource placed in our file of feelings, an essential part of our mental makeup. It's a motivator too. It is a strong, internal agitation that makes us deal with obstacles and messy situations. But the biggest problem we face is learning how to discharge it in a manner which is acceptable to society and healthy for 'the self'. For, to get angry is easy. But to get angry with the right person, to the right reason, at the right time, in the right way, is what is difficult....

Being emotional — reacting emotionally to events, news shows the level of maturity of the mind. Losing one's emotional balance is nothing but a momentary lapse into insanity. Emotional upheavals — showing excessive delight when something nice happens and showing hatred and dislike when something undesirable, unexpected happens are a strict no-no. However, one is not expected to be stoic or stony. The key is in displaying emotions to the right measure.

As we step into our workplaces, we are expected to leave our personal baggage of emotions and worries at the threshold.

So in business don't mix personal emotions. And more strictly, don't wash dirty linen in public.

Emotional equilibrium is the key for doing our duty properly without fear or favor. It is necessary not to get carried away by emotions. Emotional balance comes when the mind is well controlled. A well controlled and restrained mind is one which will not display malice in defeat or revenge in victory. Such a mind is an example of emotional stability. Haven't we seen people getting into fits of anger, get wild & violent even for silly things? What they lack is emotional stability.

Succumbing to emotional upheavals are momentary aberrations and lapse in the capacity to be rational that need an attitudinal adjustment.

Emotions play an enormous role in our lives. The reason why only the negative emotions are dealt with here is they are detrimental to our executive life-style.

Man is an emotional being. Gentlemen always know how to take care of their emotions. They never betray their emotions in public. They have superior control over their minds remaining emotionally-balanced through all conditions and circumstances. Managing emotions is nothing but displaying the maturity of mind, at its best. That way they succeed in workplaces and in life.

TABLE MANNERS

The dinner table is the center for the teaching and practicing not just of table manners but of conversation, consideration, tolerance, family feeling and just about all the other accomplishments of polite society except the minute.

—Judith Martin

Table manners are enough to judge a person. These are so elementary and basic that you must have learnt at home. But unfortunately, many executives are at a loss when it comes to adopting proper table manners while attending banquets and other official parties. Because today food and business are inseparable, table manners assume importance and are so crucial that they make or break a business deal and make a difference between getting that promotion or not.

The Formal Table Setting — Cutlery Position

- Forks will be on your left. Knives and spoons on your right.
- At the top of your plate you will find a dessert spoon and dessert fork. When dessert is served place the fork on the left and the spoon on the right.
- When eating dessert, break with the spoon and push the food with the fork into the spoon. Keep the fork in your left hand and the spoon on the right.
- A round bowl with a fairly short stem will have the glass containing red wine. Hold it at the base of the bowl.
- For white wine hold it at the base of the stem.
- Salad may be served before or after the main course of the meal. The presence of the salad fork will give you a clue.
- Finger bowls are placed after the main course or before dessert. Use the lemon slice to take oily and sticky food stuff off your hands by gently squeezing them inside the bowl. Ensure you don't splash or spill water while rinsing your fingers.

Eating

- Start eating only when your host begins or indicates you should do so.
- It is bad manners to talk with food in your mouth.
- Don't make munching sounds or belch loudly.
- Avoid chewing with an open mouth.
- Don't fill your mouth with more than you can chew. Else it will be difficult to either swallow or spit.
- Neither spit seeds or hard items nor blow your nose.
- Break larger chunks into small bits and put them into your mouth.
- Never ask for the second helping. Wait for the host to offer.

- Accept a second helping but never the third.

Posture

- Sit erect but be relaxed.
- Never place your elbows on the table until the table has been cleared away and after dinner conversation begins.
- Be careful when you extend your legs underneath the table. If you disturb anyone apologise gently.

Napkins

- Should the napkin be too large fold it into half and put it on your lap.
- Don't tuck your napkin in your neck or shirt.
- If your lap is spoiled or wet, let your host or waiter to replace them.
- Keep your napkin in your lap until you leave the table.
- Desist from using the napkin as handkerchief.
- Wiping cutlery or glassware with napkin must be avoided.

Cutlery

- Handle with care. Grip them properly for if they fall down they may break.
- If at all you break, apologize and offer to cover the cost.
- Don't try to pick up dropped spoons and cutlery from the floor. Let the waiter know and he will do it. Also don't scrap your plate clean.
- Don't push your plate away when you finish eating.
- Place your knife and fork together in the "twenty past four" position of the clock with the knife on the outside and the fork on the inside.

Passing dishes

- Pass food dishes in clock-wise direction.
- Never reach for yourself. Ask for the dish to be passed.

Emergencies

- If you get hiccups, drink plenty of water and compose yourself. Retire to the washroom if:
- You are in agony due to the lodging of hard food particles in your throat.
- Your coughing and sneezing is prolonged.

After you finish...

- Compliment if the food is excellent.
- A thank you note will be appropriate.

Be a gracious host and see that people whether they are business associates or employees are well-fed. Ask for their choice and then place the orders. Don't order more than you can eat. Be in your best behavior throughout, dignity personified since good table manners show you in new light and enhance your image as a perfect gentleman!

HOW TO BE AN OFFICIAL DIPLOMAT?

Diplomacy is the art of letting someone have your way.

—Daniele Vare

To thrive and not just survive and work our way up without leaving ruffled feathers intentionally or unintentionally we need to be diplomats in the workplace. For the times are more turbulent than ever.

Diplomats hone their communication skills so well that they can actually tell you to go to hell in such a way that you actually look forward to the trip!

Diplomats are splendid tacticians. Being tactful involves getting the timing right. Tact is knowing what to say when, and what not to ever say. Diplomacy is getting what you want without the other person feeling it let go from him.

Diplomats are excellent networkers. The first rule in diplomacy is that they follow to the letter the saying of Benjamin Franklin,

"Be civil to all, sociable to many, familiar with few, friend to one, enemy to none".

That way they acquire people management skills. A diplomat is a dealer par excellence when it comes to handling people. Diplomacy is nothing but showing a greater degree of understanding of human psychology than common folks. A diplomatic person will know the people with whom he is dealing. He understands better the drives, the desires and the demands made on the people he deals with. He is aware of the pressures that people are under and their strengths and ability, capacity and their traits.

Now what are the traits and characteristics of a diplomatic executive?

- To be a team player going with the flow is diplomatic while charting your own course away from boss's route and singing solo is not.
- Diplomatic executives never voice their concerns or resentments in public. They get things sorted out behind closed doors. Parleys are held in camera. They correct people in private.
- Diplomatic executives never play smart by superseding their superiors. To do so, they know, will be an irrevocable blunder. The right person to get your problems addressed is your boss.
- Diplomatic executives are patience personified. They never set off the alarms straight away if they see a fire. They will be meticulous in investigation leaving no stone unturned in its wake and then if necessary inform concerned people.
- They never speak all they think. But they think all they speak. Because, they know the power of words and the ability of them to hurt people, albeit unintentionally. They exercise the greatest caution in choosing their words.
- Diplomats never blow off all they have in one go. They don't fire all the bullets they have.
- They play their cards well keeping them close to their chest. They are men of few words and hence it will be difficult to fathom them to bring out what's going in behind the head.
- A diplomat's actions speak for him. They are not the

type of guys who will say and do but rather do and say.

- They know the rules of the game so well that they play to win both ways. They are careful about the company they keep and bother much about with whom they must be seen with and with whom not.
- Diplomats know the value of silence and the powers of observation. They simply following this dictum "Keep your mouth shut and eyes open".
- Diplomats are excellent listeners. From listening comes wisdom, and from speaking repentance.
- By their words, demeanor, actions they let people that they mean business. So that others will not play with them.
- They don't play fast and loose. Their actions and words will be very well coordinated.
- Diplomats play safe always. They never talk anything in the face, nor do they point an accusing finger at people. They betray no emotion even under grave provocation. They are masters in self-control.
- Diplomatic executives never pick up quarrels like common folks. They don't argue to convince others to see their viewpoint. Instead of pushing the other side towards an agreement, they draw them in the direction they want them to move.
- They never bad-mouth people, indulge in seditious activities and are not seen in gossip circles.

However diplomacy does mean that one may smile, and smile, and be villain. Diplomacy is being tactful and getting things done. There lies the power of a diplomat. And diplomatic executives are high-flyers and they don't have anything to lose but everything to gain if they only care to be a bit tactful! And that's the way to be the official diplomat!

TREATING VISITORS

Who is the most important person to you?
The person who is sitting in front of me.

You might be wondering why on such a mundane and common topic a discussion is made. On the first place, do we need a discussion at all? Read on and you'll understand why. In business, just as in your personal life, visitors must be treated well. For the way you treat them reflects your image and that of your company.

- Don't keep business visitors waiting more than necessary. Remember they too have to mind about a thousand other tasks like you.
- Offer them a seat and ensure that they are comfortable.
- Be business-like while meeting visitors. Get straight to the point. Don't mix personal problems in your meeting.
- But personalise your meeting with him to the extent that the visitor feels good to see you. Build an image and reputation for yourself as the best host in your company. A stiff upper lip attitude will not help.
- Make eye-contact and speak clearly.
- When a visitor is sitting in front of you, bear in mind that he is the most important person to you for the time being. With your decision to let a visitor to meet you, keep away from files and papers. Devote your entire time and time in finishing your business with the visitor. So avoid distractions like attending phone calls, checking e-mails, etc.

In the words of Dr. Richard Moss,

> "The greatest gift you can give another is the purity of your attention".

- Ensure that you offer your visitors something to refresh themselves. A soft drink or hot beverage goes beyond basic courtesy. A toffee lightens up people.
- Avoid entertaining friends at your office. If you do that your reputation goes for a toss.

- Be conscious of the time. Keep your meeting short but purposeful.
- Its bad manners to smoke or chew in front of your visitors.
- Don't think that you can enhance your image and show off your authority by taking employees to task in front of your visitors or appearing 'busy' with work.
- If unable to entertain a visitor, take a few moments off from your job and meet him in person, apologise and explain the reason. Arrange to fix the meeting at a later date. Be specific and sound sincere.
- When your visitor is superior to you rise from your seat as he arrives and greet.
- Every visitor would appreciate greatly if you give them a warm send-off walking up to your room's threshold. But extend this gesture only to people whom you value most.
- If you have to attend some urgent business mid-way, excuse yourself and don't forget to get back to finish the business with your visitor. Don't let the visitor to take French leave.

After meeting you, your visitors must feel glad and be thankful to you for giving them an opportunity to interact. With the fulfillment of their jobs or finding you responsive to them they should carry good impressions about you and your company.

As a busy and responsible executive, it may be just another of your routine business visitor. But for him such meetings would be a great job done well and feel satisfied if you treat him with courtesy and politeness that are the hallmarks of a perfect gentleman!

THE ART OF CONVERSATION

Conversation makes one what he is

For almost all of us conversing is as easy as a duck taking to water. But very few are regarded as good conversationalists. The reason is that not everyone has mastered the art of conversation. You might be wondering whether it is worth to invest your time and energy to know how to converse. Yet it has its own advantages and merits to learn this skill.

Diplomats are people who know well the charm and power of art of conversation. Here we discuss in brief about this skill which is pertinent to business executives. Owing to the lack of knowledge about the nuances of conversation many people get into awkward tight-corners by saying wrong things at right places.

The Basics

Before you start conversing with others, there are a few things that are to be taken care of.

1. Smile

A man without a smiling face must not open a shop.

—Chinese proverb

Smile. It creates an instant rapport with others. It generates confidence and people like to speak and be spoken to them by persons who sport a smile, as opposed to persons who have a stiff upper lip. It wouldn't be far fetched when I say that if you don't smile, you are headed for trouble. A smile is the first means to market yourself to others. A smile says, "I like you. You make me happy. I am glad to see you".

2. Know your ABC

Always be courteous. Be polite throughout your conversation. Politeness makes conversations a pleasant affair. It reflects your maturity of mind and portrays you as a well-groomed person. People like talking to polite persons. Don't go looking out for fights. Does anyone like to carry on with a rough and tough guy?

3. Be Positive and Friendly

Have an open mind. Don't allow prejudices to cloud your mind. Encourage others to talk. Always nurture positive thoughts before you begin conversing. Watch your attitude since it is the first thing people notice about you.

Be friendly. The next person you meet may become your best friend. Friendliness begets friendship.

4. Don't be Talkative

He cannot speak well, that cannot hold his tongue. Talkative persons neither hear nor learn. Talkative people are not welcome everywhere. "That man's silence is wonderful to hear" shouldn't be the refrain from others. Talk when you must. More than anything else, in conversations, allow the other person to talk. He will feel happy to get a chance to put his views across.

5. Be a Diplomat

There is an old saying, "Speech is the picture of the mind". Be tactful in your conversation. Never point directly to anyone's mistakes. If you have to, draw attention in an indirect way. Speak about pleasant topics.

6. Clarity

Clarity of thought and speech go hand in hand. Both are required to carry on a conversation. Speak clearly without being ambiguous. You must possess good command of the language, well-read so that you can participate in any topic and get the pronunciation right. Watch your accent closely. It should not be influenced by your mother tongue or region. Heavily-accented English doesn't sound fine. Develop an accent which is neutral and nice to hear.

Six ways to make people like you

Celebrated author Dale Carnegie prescribes the following to make people like you.

1. Become genuinely interested in other people.
2. Smile.
3. Call people by their names. Remember that a man's name is to him the sweetest and most important sound in any language.
4. Be a good listener. Encourage others to talk about themselves.
5. Talk in terms of the other man's interests.
6. Make the other person feel important and do it sincerely.

The ground rules for being a good conversationalist

1. Avoid name dropping. It paints a poor picture of you.
2. Listen to others. By listening comes wisdom.
3. Don't discuss your personal problems and your health status. In short, as the saying goes, "Don't wash your dirty linen in public".
4. Neither ask a man his salary nor a woman her age.
5. Desist from asking the price of jewellery, clothing and personal effects.
6. Restrain yourself from sounding pompous and using bombastic language. It puts off many people.
7. Don't monopolise the conversation. A good conversationalist will give time for the other person to talk.
8. Don't tell questionable jokes. Eg. Racist jokes may hurt others.
9. Don't try to show off your wealth, knowledge or the places you have travelled in your conversation.
10. If someone asks questions which you don't wish to answer, reply, "I don't know" or change the subject subtly.
11. If you don't have ready answers don't try to mislead others by giving false or wrong ones. Admit your ignorance and assure them to get the answers right some time later.
12. Modulate your voice accordingly.
13. Don't swear or take extreme positions.
14. Never enquire about physical handicaps.
15. Never ask professional questions to doctors, lawyers and tax consultants in a social setting.
16. Don't criticise, back-bite someone who is not present. Never talk ill of others.
17. Don't ask people about their personal affairs like their clothing size, age, weight, etc.

18. Don't draw comparisons between different people particularly if they are present.
19. Focus on what the person is saying rather than your own thoughts.
20. Nod and maintain eye contact throughout your conversation.
21. Interject vocal cues like "Fine", "Then what happened", "Good" to show that you are listening.
22. Ask open-ended questions to allow the person to prolong the conversation.
23. Ask close-ended questions, those which can be answered with "Yes" or "No" to bring conversation to an end.
24. Use the person's name along with the title often when you address him.
25. Never let out secrets. For they are sensitive and sacred and it amounts to betrayal.
26. Speak error-free language. But don't correct anyone's language.
27. Don't dispute when you hear someone giving wrong information. Just say, "I thought..."
28. Use dignified language. Avoid using slang or colloquial language.
29. Move on to the next group in a subtle way and join the other in an equally subtle manner. Staying in the same group throughout will cause boredom.
30. Don't bulldoze your way through a group. Get in only if you feel welcomed.
31. Don't impose your views and opinions upon others. Every one is entitled to have his.
32. Never lose your temper even at the gravest of provocations in a social setting. Take care not to shout or whine.
33. Avoid getting into arguments. You can't win an argumentative person.
34. Never contest or contradict anyone's opinions. Be a man of consensus not a man of confrontation. A

gentleman would give space for manoeuvre allowing the other person to save his face.

35. Avoid sarcasm and nose cuts with stinging remarks. It's rude to do so.
36. Focus on the positive aspects. Not on negative aspects.

Topics for Conversation

Often we are caught off guard when we are about to start conversing in a social setting. We are at a loss to know what topics are to be discussed, those which are safe and liked by everybody. Find a topic which is of common interest to everyone and start.

Apart from topics of mutual or common interest, weather and inflation can be safe bets.

Topics to Avoid

Saying wrong things at the right place can tarnish your image among people. So beware of topics which you should never initiate.

Never broach topics about which people feel sensitive and too personal. Topics about war, former colonial powers, politics, race and religion will head you to trouble. Steer clear of these topics as well as all controversial ones.

Variety is the Spice of Life

In conversations too this maxim holds good. Don't harp on the same topic throughout your talk. Think of different topics of common interest beforehand and subtly move over from one topic to another. For the listeners get bored if you hold on to one topic for long. A wide range of topic interests everyone and it is a joy for everyone to participate in such conversations. Moreover, discussing a variety of topics will throw up new facts hitherto unknown to people and as such it is an informative and rewarding experience.

Never Argue

A person who argues constantly will never be a good conversationalist.

Benjamin Franklin says, "If you argue and rankle and contradict, you may achieve a victory sometimes: but it will be an empty victory because you will never get your opponent's good will".

In the words of Abraham Lincoln, "No man who is resolved to make the most of himself, can spare time for personal contention. Still less can he afford to take the consequences, including the vitiation of his temper and loss of self-control. Yield larger things to which you show no more than equal rights; and yield less ones through clearly your own. Better give your path to a dog than be bitten by him in contesting for the right. Even killing the dog would not cure the bite".

Understand one thing for sure: Arguments lead you nowhere. You only get bitter and frustrated. Arguing never wins your case. You are just wasting your time by fighting a losing battle.

Six Golden Rules

Learn to say the following in your day-to-day conversations with people:

1. Sorry — when you are wrong.
2. Thank You — when you receive help from others.
3. Will you please? — when you want something to get things done by others.
4. What is your opinion? — Give chance for others, trying not to impose your views.
5. You did a good job! — when you find someone who has done well.
6. I admit I made a mistake — when you commit a mistake.

And now see for yourself the results they get when you start using in day-to-day conversation.

Having got to know about the nuances of the art of conversation you must feel confident of making yourself comfortable with anyone. A good conversationalist is a person who is loved by all and is most welcome at all social occasions. Put this skill into use in every opportunity that comes your way. Eventually you will begin enjoying conversing with people. There is no looking back once you are at ease with yourself than before. And as the saying goes, "Education begins a gentleman, conversation completes him!"

Technology Etiquette

Gentlemen are tech-savvy

Thanks to the advancements in technology, today communication is not at all a problem. However, the effectiveness of communication lies in the way we use them. Many people, even seasoned professionals, lack what is known as technology etiquette. This just teaches how best we can leverage our communication skills with the technology mediums available to us in our workplace.

TELEPHONE SKILLS

The effectiveness of a telephone conversation is in inverse proposition to the time spent on it.

—Parkinson's Law of the Telephone

We just can't imagine life without a telephone. Let's first get it right that a telephone is to be used only for short durations and not for chitchatting. We misuse the telephone to the extent the call stretches itself for more than an hour. In some companies, executives even call their branch offices located in the other end of the country to tally accounts entry-by-entry without realizing that the expense incurred is well enough to make a trip in person to do the same job. Brevity is the watchword of telephone conversations. Here is where we need to learn some skills what is popularly called as Telephone Skills.

Generally Speaking

1. Place your telephone nearby where you work so that it is handy. Ideally, it should be within your arm's reach.
2. Keep a pen and scribbling pad near to your phone so that you can take notes while talking without wasting time searching for them.
3. Start your talk immediately and don't indulge in small talk. While conducting business you need to get to

the point at once. By saying, “How did you spend your weekend?”, “What did you have for breakfast?” you are only wasting precious time and money. You are also setting a bad example to your people.

4. Speak clearly and in normal manner so that what you say is audible to the other person. Don’t shout or whisper.
5. Don’t munch, chew or smoke while speaking over the phone.
6. Keep the handset near your mouth and not away.
7. Cover the mouthpiece if you have to talk to someone else mid-way and bear in mind that the caller can still hear you. If available, use the Flash facility of your telephone to deter the other person from hearing noises while waiting.
8. If you can’t make out what the other person is saying politely ask him to repeat. Never assume for it you could get him wrong.
9. Listen attentively and let the caller know you are paying attention with vocal equivalent of facial expression and body language: “Yes”, “Fine”, “I see”, “OK”.
10. Modulate your voice since the other person is unable to see your expressions and your only way to make yourself clear is through voice modulation.
11. Speak in your normal pace. Neither too fast nor too slow.
12. Read the user’s manual of your telephone and make full use of the features mentioned therein.
13. When you are asked to wait don’t show your annoyance.
14. When passing numbers repeat them twice or better still thrice. Ensure that the other person got it right. Do the same when you have got to write down numbers.
15. Be brief and be up to the point for you may be wasting the other person’s time. Also important calls

others may be making cannot come through when you are hooked upto the phone.

16. While speaking over the phone put off music or any other noisy appliances. If not possible, get away from noisy places.
17. Avoid eavesdropping. Its poor manners to do so. If someone is talking on the phone get away from there. If impossible, try to concentrate on other things like reading paper. Appear concentrating on books, computers. The point here is you should give the impression that you are not overhearing.
18. While ending your conversation put down the handset gently. Never slam it down. Also ensure to put back the receiver in its place properly.

When you Call Someone

1. Before placing calls, list out the points you are going to speak in a paper.
2. When making a call, first ensure that the person whom you are calling is on the line and start your conversation with pleasantries. Never say "Who is that?" or "Who is on the line?" when you call someone. People get irritated and annoyed. Just think for yourself how you will feel when someone calls you at your office and questions who you are.
3. If you haven't been able to reach the person ask when it would be fine to call.
4. Don't ask where the person is when he or she is not available.
5. If you dial the wrong number, apologise and hang up.
6. Always ask if it is a convenient time to call.
7. Be polite when calling a friend in his business place. Your friend's reputation is at stake.
8. Speak clearly when leaving message on an answering machine and give the date, time, name, company number and your message in a brief manner. Don't grunt, chuckle or laugh. Nor let any time lags in your message.

9. Call employees at home only when it is absolutely necessary but be brief.
10. Take advantage of off-peak reduced rates. This way you save money.

When the Call is for You

1. Answer your telephone before the third ring and greet in a business-like way.
2. Identify yourself with your full name/designation.
3. Smile while picking up the phone. The caller will hear it in your voice.
4. Let the caller to hang up and never yourself.
5. If people call you when it is inconvenient like when you are in a rush, tell the caller politely but to assure them that you would call back later.
6. If you are going to be away, get someone to take calls on your behalf. Continuously ringing phone indicates a lack of personal organization. Make it a point to call people who rang up when you were away.
7. When you want to attend something mid-way through your call, politely excuse yourself, attend to it quickly and don't forget to get back to the phone.
8. When you take calls that are not routed via the exchange board, tell your company name first and then enquire with a polite "May I help you?"

And finally, never think that you can substitute your physical presence with a phone call.

CELL PHONE SKILLS

Cell phones are ubiquitous fixtures these days. Just like the telephone, while using the cell phone some manners and etiquette needs to be adopted along with telephone skills.

1. Place the cell phone in such a way that what you speak is audible to the other person.
2. Avoid taking calls while you are driving. Let the caller know and call later.

3. Stop your vehicle and talk. Never drive talking on the cell with one hand and driving with the other. Cell phone induced accidents are on the rise.
4. Switch off cell phones while traveling by air since the transmission relays of the aircraft to the ground ATC will be hindered by the waves emanating from the cell phone.
5. People having pacemakers in their heart must avoid using cell phone as it may affect the effective functioning of it.
6. Keep away from cell phones when lightning strikes with the rain. The cell phone, due to its metal parts, attracts lightning which may be detrimental to the safety of the people carrying them.
7. Never use cell phones at hospitals particularly near operation theaters.
8. Turn your cell phone into vibrator mode whenever you attend meetings or training sessions.
9. Keep your cell phone switched on always. It could be irritating for callers to get pre-recorded messages informing about your inaccessibility. The very purpose of carrying the cell phone "Anywhere-Anytime Contact" is defeated.
10. Charge your cell phone's batteries periodically. Cell phone downtime should be kept to the minimum or better still, nil.

Cell phones should be used with discretion. It should be at the same time be of great help and ease in communication and yet not be an inconvenience, irritation or disturb the environment. So fine tune your act when using your cell phone.

VIDEO-CONFERENCING SKILLS

With video-conferencing gaining ground as a popular medium to effectively communicate with people across great distances, some skills are to be learnt to make it more productive session.

The Spadework

1. List out and know about the participants before the session.
2. Set the goals and purposes of the video-conference.
3. Send information brochure, handouts in advance via e-mail to the participants so that the discussion will be meaningful.
4. Keep writing instruments, scribbling pads handy.
5. Place a technician as a stand-by to troubleshoot technical snags, if any.
6. Keep the telephone and fax nearby within arm's reach.

Attire and Appearance

1. Sport a professional look.
2. Don't wear jewellery, junk or real, that glint or sparkle in the light.
3. Avoid wearing clothes which are flashy and gaudy. Wear clothes which are moderate in color so as to avoid projecting distorted images with poor clarity.

Presenting yourself

1. Remember to look straight into the lens of the camera to maintain eye contact. It gives the impression of establishing a direct, one-to-one interaction with the other participants.
2. Be comfortable with the devices and camera.
3. Over-gesturing will be distracting to viewers.
4. Position yourself correctly before the camera so that your face is fully visible and is projected without distortions and.
5. Clarity in speech and thought is necessary. Perfect your tone, pronunciation and diction.
6. What you say matters a lot. Choose your words with care and ensure that you convey the right message.
7. Don't let time lags during the session.
8. Make it an interactive session to sustain interest and participation.

Mike manners

1. Switch off your microphone when none is speaking on your side since it will deter sending unnecessary sounds.
2. Keep disturbing sounds to the minimum. Avoid tapping pens, foot, shuffling papers, coughing, switch off whirring fans etc
3. Speak clearly by keeping the microphone at correct distance. Neither too close nor too far. If not your voice will be distorted.

Finally, for a productive session don't let yourself to be disturbed. Instruct your people to put on hold phone calls and switch off your cell phones.

Become tech-savvy and you will eventually ease out in using modern communication gadgets and systems. And those who have excellent technology etiquette, without doubt, qualify to become the perfect gentleman!

5

PERSONALITY DEVELOPMENT

Re-invent your personality

- Seven Qualities of Successful People
  - (1) Goal Setting — Think Big, Dream Big, Achieve Big
  - (2) See Beyond the Horizon
  - (3) Positive Thinking — Positive Living
  - (4) Failure is Never Final
  - (5) The Winning Edge
  - (6) Attitude is Everything
  - (7) Belief in Oneself
- Image-building — Your Personal Brand Identity

Man's main task in life is to give birth to himself, to become what he potentially is. The most important product of his effort is his own personality

—Erich Fromm

Personality Development — It is one facet of human development that schools and colleges neglect to teach. No wonder, it is one aspect every individual in general and every job aspirant in particular strives to achieve long after finishing college. That is one reason why there is so much craze over 'personality development' courses conducted in posh hotels spending a fortune in acquiring them. It is understandable why people particularly youngsters, develop such profound interest in developing their personalities. For it is clear to see — persons who have developed their personalities succeed in their career than others.

Personality Evolves

However, personality development cannot be 'acquired' just by attending courses over a week or by reading half-a-dozen best sellers. In fact, none can develop their personality overnight. Developing your personality is not a one-time effort. It is an on-going, ever-evolving process which can be achieved only through constant efforts.

PD Never Stops

Books and courses will give you some thoughts and leads by which you and you alone will have to proceed further based on those ideas and thoughts. One way to develop personality is to become an avid life-long student of people and their behavior. By emulating worthy people, keenly observing different people and analyzing various facets of famous personalities one can gain some success in developing their personalities. None can claim that he has attained the optimum of his personality development endeavors. It is a life-long process and as such personality development never stops.

Invest

Everyone wants to develop their personalities so as to present themselves as persons of substance in this highly competitive job market or corporate machine. Developing your personality requires considerable amount of time, effort and at times resources and you must be prepared for that.

Total Personality Development

· *Always remember that your personality is your big asset. Do not try to emulate another person. Real personality comes from the heart.*

—Thomas J. Watson

Before we proceed further, let's get it right with the exact meaning or what the term 'personality development' really connotes. It is a wide-spread fallacy and commonly held view that personality means external appearance and a person's looks. Really personality doesn't mean this alone. It goes beyond a person's visage and countenance. One shouldn't judge people merely by external factors alone. Unfortunately, that's what happens in reality. Looks and appearances are God-given. None can change it substantially. Can you really change your face? Of course, it can happen with make-up and plastic surgeries. But they are merely cosmetic. What counts really as personality is much more.

Personality doesn't mean the physical aspect alone. Personality Development aims at all-round development of all aspects of human life — physical, mental, moral and spiritual. These four different dimensions of human personality have to be nurtured with care for a harmonious growth. Each one of these aspects is important and one cannot downplay the value of them. Neglecting even one of them would always be a shortcoming and personality development can never be complete without it. That is total personality development.

Real personality evolves based on the strength of character. Not by cosmetics, high-flying lifestyle, position or the wealth one flaunts. Bear in mind that character alone is the bed-rock of strong personality. And such personalities earn undying fame and goodwill from people who they come across. It is those strong personalities who spell success. Seriously study such people and emulate them.

Personality transcends beyond images and appearances. It delves deeper into a person — his attitude towards people and the world, values and principles he holds, the ambitions and goals he aims for, receptivity to new ideas, modern in thinking, the outlook he nurtures towards life and finally his entire frame of mind or mental set up with which he takes the vicissitudes that life batters him with.

Personality Development is an enigmatic topic with no boundaries. To achieve your optimum you will have to embark on a long journey in your bid to acquire certain qualities and skills so as to develop your personality to a great extent, if not fully.

Practise, Practise, Practise!

Above all, mere reading will not be of help. It all depends much on how much you exert yourself — some conscious self-efforts from your side in acquiring required skills and knowledge towards developing your personality and in that endeavor not leaving no stone unturned for sure. Putting into practice what you hear, read and observe in your daily life until they become a habit, a way of life for good. Little gestures on your part would greatly enhance your personality.

Finally, to develop your personality in whatever you do strive for perfection but settle for excellence. It is those people who have well-developed personalities get to the top in their career in a short time. You can start transforming at any time of your career.

Re-invent your personality by changing your outlook and attitude towards things. For this to happen, just as told before, you and you alone have to take some visible efforts on your part so as to make a real change and move forward to sport a strong and well-developed personality!

Goal Setting —
Think Big, Dream Big, Achieve Big

Know where you are going. The great thing in the world is not so much where we stand, as in what direction we are moving.

—Oliver Wendell Holmes

Without goals you are nowhere. Where you start and where you end is defined by the goals you have in your life. The destination begins your journey; a goal begins your endeavor. All progress starts with a meaningful goal in mind.

Goals Definition

First define your goals. Setting goals give us a sense of purpose and mission. With goal setting you get your priorities right. You gain a sense of direction while moving on.

Experts say goals must be SMART — Specific, Measurable, Achievable, Realistic, Time-bound.

Specific — Get down to specifics while setting goals. Vague goals will lead you nowhere. As the saying goes, if you run after two hares, you will catch neither.

Measurable — Goals should be measurable. Our progress evaluation is possible only when our goals are measurable. The action plan for achieving every goal must have various milestones which help us to monitor our progress.

Achievable — Your ability to achieve the goals can be determined by SWOT — Strengths, Weaknesses, Opportunities and Threats analysis.

Graham Green's words explain, "Despair is the price one pays for setting oneself an impossible aim." Attempt nothing beyond your strength. Don't stretch yourself too thin.

Realistic — People get carried away by being too optimistic to forget the realities. It's like an officer wanting to become chairman of the corporation in two years. Know your limits, your means and set goals.

Time-bound — Goals are dreams with deadlines. Goal accomplishment will be certain only when you set a target time and date. Without them there is nothing to self-direct and automatically control your activities towards realization of goals.

Why Goals?

If one advances confidently in the direction of their dreams, and endeavors to live a life which they have imagined, they will meet with a success unexpected in common hours.

—Henry David Thoreau

The purpose of goals is to focus our attention. The mind will not reach towards achievements until it has clear objectives. Without goals to guide us we will be merely wandering here and there; not travelling towards our destination.

Goal setting culminates in the accomplishment of goals. The logical end of this process of goal setting ends up in realization of the goals. For this to happen, there must be some conscious efforts and activities on our part towards achievement of goals. There lies the efficacy of goal setting.

Setting goals is nothing but a promise you make with yourself. Fulfilment of that promise comes when you follow up goal setting with action on ground so as to make progress — incremental it may be though, towards the set goals. Good promises end up in good performances.

How to Achieve Goals?

It is not enough to aim; you must hit!

The answer is simple: work towards it. It is easier said than done. It's easy for everyone to set goals. But what's difficult is achieving them.

Action on ground is necessary to make our progress towards goals. Again mere activity will not help. If you have observed the activities of dogs you will understand better. A dog will keep on running as if it's got a mission to achieve. But it's nothing to do and keeps on running. There is a saying, "Dogs have no work yet they don't have the time to stop".

Action that is result-oriented is essential to achieve goals. Every activity you undertake should conform to the statement of purpose and ultimately lead you to fulfill the goals. Without action, goals are unfulfilled dreams

Write Out Your Goals

One strategy most achievers suggest is to write down your goals along with the time-frame. Have a statement of purpose written and it will serve as a road map towards achieving goals. Just imagine if you want to learn a new language within one year put it down in writing. If you don't, that one year will always be one year even though you planned it 3 months ago!

As such, goals that aren't written down aren't goals at all. They are mere wishes.

Commitment

This one step — choosing a goal and sticking to it — changes everything.

—Scott Reed

Commitment towards your goals is absolutely necessary to realise them. If you are committed you will not easily think of giving up when things get rough.

Commitment strengthens your resolve and the result is tenacity. Obstacles will only serve as stepping stones in your pursuit of goals.

Review

Every plan's objective is to achieve some goals. As such goals are our plans for the future. Constantly monitor the distance you cover and get back on track whenever you deviate. Reviewing periodically should become a habit. Every milestone you cross should become a stepping stone in your forward march towards achievement of goals. As such milestones you reach must serve as a motivating factor.

High Goals; High Results

Think little goals and expect little achievements.
Think big goals and win big success.

—Unknown

Our perception towards goals must undergo a sea change. We always settle for goals that are easy and quick to realise. Always look for setting goals that are bigger than you are. Perceive every goal that you dream to achieve with belief and determination no matter however big they may be. You are sure to attain your goals.

'Think Big, Dream Big, Achieve Big' must become a way of life. He who aims at the moon may hit the tip of a tree; he who aims at the top of a tree is unlikely to get off the ground. That's the rationale behind 'Think Big, Dream Big, Achieve Big'.

Get the best; leave the rest. If your goal makes you to exert yourself a bit, then chances are that you have really good goal — one that will stretch you to the optimum bringing out the best of you!

Goals serve as the beacon light to which we have to make progress. Your destination is the goal; your route is the plan.

Goals should help you to make progress — both in your personal and professional lives. As such goals must be meaningful and in concert with the values and principles you cherish.

It is said that the secret of success is the constancy to purpose. And to high goals too! So "Think Big, Dream Big, Achieve Big" to get make a big deal out of life!

Lazy laggards have 'hopes'
Common folks have 'wishes'
Brave fellows have 'ambitions'
Only a few great ones are after 'a goal & purpose in life!'
If wishes were horses, everyone will go for a ride!

See Beyond the Horizon

THE BIG PICTURE

See the whole picture; adjust the lens
To see the stars far and deep.
Let the wide angle admit
All of life's light and shadows.

See the whole picture; Focus the mind's eye
Like a spotlight on the inner stage.
Only with eyes shut tight
Can there be the brilliant insight.

See the whole picture; Scan the edges,
For meaning may not lie in the center.
As the sculpture is revealed in its form
And the sea is defined by its shore.

See the whole picture; Study the dreams
Of the great dreamers and sages.
Thus did Martin, through Gandhi's eyes,
See freedom in Montgomery's masses
Now —
See the whole picture.

—Author Unknown

Perhaps you must have heard a popular anecdote in management literature. It happened so that there were three people working in a construction site. A man walked upto the first man enquired as to what the workman was doing. He told that he was laying the bricks. To the same question the second man replied that he was building a wall. The third man responded that he was building a cathedral. You can see for yourself how three people saw different things while doing the same job according to their outlook and mental vision.

The irony is people are so short-sighted that they see the trees missing out the forest. See the whole picture. Look ahead. See beyond the horizon.

Positive Thinking — Positive Living

Think you can; think you can't. Either way you're right.

—Henry Ford

To survive and thrive in this ever-changing, complex and competitive world it needs a lot more than ability and skills. Positive thinking is the most fundamental trait in every successful person. Mind you, negative or positive — one of these can make you or break you, depending on what you choose.

Team Up with Positive

A man is known and shaped by the company he keeps. With positive people he gets positive influences, with negative people he gets negative influences. The company of restless people makes you restless. Similarly, negative people make you negative. It is as simple as that.

Team up with high-energy, ambitious people. They think of possibilities to achieve their endeavors. Their mentality will be infectious. It will help in developing a positive mindset.

"If It's to Be, It's Up to Me"

The two most power-filled words are "I can" and the two most debilitating words is "I can't". The choice to just knock the "t" off the 'can't' depends on your mentality; not your ability. It is pertinent to nurture the right frame of mind. Positive thinking sets you on the path of progress.

The Importance of Thoughts

21st century is being touted as the 'thought attack century' just as 20th century was called as the 'heart attack century'. Thoughts are fundamental to our existence. What Buddha said ages ago is still relevant today.

"We are what we think
All that we are arises
With our thoughts
We make our world".

The wish is father to the thought. We soon believe what we desire. So believe in the possible and be positive.

Nurture Positive Thoughts

Nurturing positive thoughts is vital for forging positive relationships with people and the way in which others perceive us when they come in contact with us. There is a story in Indian mythology to illustrate the power and the effect of positive thinking.

It so happened that a king used to pass by a certain street in his chariot on his way to the Court. Every day people and the shopkeepers used to bow and salute him. The king reciprocated the same and went on his way. But on one particular day he felt an aversion to respond to a sandal wood merchant who bowed before him. The same feeling enveloped the king for the next few days. Perplexed how he could feel bad about an unknown citizen, the king met a sage and explained his predicament.

The wise sage asked the king to purchase the entire stock of sandal wood from the merchant's shop and report back after a week. The king did as told and came back to the sage to narrate how he felt on seeing the merchant — glad just as before. The sage listened and explained that the merchant previously worried about his sluggish business and wished if the king is dead all his stock would be bought for his funeral and he can make some money. At that point of time, the king's mind had been attacked by the negative thoughts of the merchant and naturally he felt an aversion to him. On the other hand, when the king purchased the entire stock on the sage's advice the merchant felt happy and wished the king well. This time the king had no ill-feeling and was just as before!

So understand how thought waves affect people. When you have negative thoughts about people their response is hostile towards you. With positive thoughts their response is warm and cordial!

Think Positive

The environment you fashion of out of — your thoughts — your beliefs — your ideals — your philosophy — is the only climate you will ever live in.

—Alfred A. Montaperi

All confidence is acquired or self-developed through positive thinking, which is triggered off by good books, good friends and good visits.

Thinking positive stonewalls negativity. Tune in your positive antenna and condition yourself to think positively. Be an optimist a die-hard one at that. Die-hard optimists don't get easily discouraged by the scenario or the initial setbacks.

To paraphrase what they say about winners,

"Optimists don't see different things, they see things differently".

Little wonder, winners are basically die-hard optimists.

When you think positive the possibilities are infinite — Think you can do it. What one sees as a problem someone see as an opportunity and challenge. Our attitude is shaped by the way we look at things. Let our views be positive.

The Art of Possibility Thinking

The habit of looking on the best side of every event is worth more than a thousand pounds a year

—Dr Samuel Johnson

Believe in the art of possibility thinking. When you sell an idea to kids and say "It's big and tough" they will counter with, "Why not?" Children believe in the possible and they want to try out before giving up. Ignorance is bliss. They are blind to any perception about hindrances. The opposite is the mentality of grown-ups. We see obstacles where none existed and never attempt.

Positive thoughts change the very pattern of our thinking. When patterns are broken, new worlds emerge.

At first sight, every problem looks formidable. Don't chicken out. Nothing is as tough as it looks. Approach and try out first with positive attitude and you will be at ease. Developing positive thinking and the ability to view at things positively gives you the firepower to get you started. Just imagine if all us think of impossibilities in our endeavors we wouldn't have come this far at all. So far we have travelled unconsciously. Now to confront bigger challenges let's do it consciously.

Take on the world with positive thinking. That gives you the right frame of mind — the confidence and the resolve to carry on undaunted. Apply positive thinking consistently in every endeavor. And the world will be at your feet only if you learn and master this art of positive thinking — positive living.

The Optimist Creed

Promise yourself:

- To be strong that nothing can disturb your peace of mind.
- To talk about happiness and prosperous to every person you meet.
- To make all your friends feel that there is something in them.
- To look at the sunny side of everything and make your optimism come true.
- To think only of the best to work only for the best and to expect only the best.
- To be just as enthusiastic about the success of others as you are about your own.
- To forget the mistakes of the past and press on the greater achievements of the future.
- To wear a cheerful countenance at all times and give every living creature you meet a smile.
- To give so much time to the improvement of yourself that you have no time to criticize others.
- To be large for worry, too noble for anger, too strong for fear, and too happy to permit the presence of trouble.

—Anon

Failure is Never Final

Failure happens only once — when you stop trying to succeed.

When you fall down what you need to do is to pick yourself up, dust yourself off and carry on. This simple yet determined act of a spider is what exactly inspired and gave hope and courage, centuries ago to Robert Bruce to win his kingdom back.

The first step to emerge out of failure unscathed is to overcome tendencies that hold you back. Try again till you succeed. Simply, there shouldn't be any stops to success. Perhaps, failure came to you because you have left stones unturned. Pause, take stock and try again.

One failure and that's the end of all our endeavors. This seems to be the philosophy of many people. Don't get put off one failure. There is more to do in life rather than get bogged down by one silly failure.

Managing failure is crucial to beat away the blues and emerge unscathed psychologically. And most importantly, understand that failure management's logical end is success achievement.

The Genesis of Failures

If you carefully introspect on failures — yours or others, one unmistakable factor emerges — mistakes. It wouldn't be wrong to say that every failure, big or small, was caused due mistakes, one or a host of them.

So, mistakes are the genesis of failures and as such take measures to avoid making mistakes. Though achieving zero-mistakes is next to impossible, yet one should take cognizance of the fact that such a proposition remains within the realm of possibility. Or on the other hand, if mistakes happen ensure that they aren't costly ones, for rectifying the same would be futile. The reasons for such futility of rectifications could be due to irrelevance (like 'medicine after the patient is dead') or inability to get on track even after correction. Costly errors are best avoided since they exact a huge price for correction. And the road to normalcy isn't easy either.

However, there is no point in spending one's time & energy in brooding or regretting. View mistakes as opportunity to learn and ensure that you don't commit the same mistake again.

Associate with Positive People

Negative people are akin to Indian crabs. Neither they go up nor allow you to go up. Perhaps you will be knowing the nature of these crabs which pull down each other whenever one tries to climb out of the basket in which they are kept. Fishermen never close these baskets since they know very well that none will be missing.

There was a frog who wanted to participate in a running race. The race track wound its way atop a hill. Many animals joined the race only to drop out mid-way unable to bear the exhaustion of climbing a hill. But seeing the frog hopping on with gusto the audience began to jeer. They kept telling him, "You will never make it. You are only a frog" and so on. Yet the frog carried on relentlessly. Finally it won the race. The audience crowded around him and wondered, "How did you go on despite our discouragement?" All the while the frog kept smiling. Only later someone figured out that the frog was deaf! Be deaf to negative people.

Negative people spread negative thoughts. With positive people optimism is contagious. So choose your company with great care.

Never Give Up!

Success consists of going from failure to failure without loss of enthusiasm.

—Sir Winston Churchill

Failure can be gut-wrenching, discouraging and confidence-shattering. Surrendering to frustrations is fatal. Gear up for a long haul. Perhaps no article on this topic is ever complete without the mention of the life-story of this man which convinces us the values of courage, persistence and perseverance. Such is the inspirational power of his life's failures and accomplishments hold.

Events	**Age**
He failed in business	22
He ran for the State Legislature and was defeated	23
Business failure again	24
Elected to the State Legislature	25
His sweetheart died	26
Suffered nervous breakdown	27
Defeated for the position of House Speaker	29
Defeated for the position of Elector	31

Defeated for the Congress	34
Elected to the Congress	37
Defeated for the Congress	39
Defeated for the Senate	46
Defeated for the Vice-Presidency	47
Again defeated for the Senate	49
Elected President of the United States	51

That man was Abraham Lincoln, considered to be the greatest President, the US ever had. He is one rare person who believed he can even in the face of repeated defeats and in the end won. His story illustrates the fact that one must never stop trying. You are not yet a failure until you quit. So never give up!

Can You be Failure-proof?

Don't fear failure so much that you refuse to try new things. The saddest summary of a life contains three descriptions: could have, might have, and should have.

—Louis E. Boone

The answer to this question is a big NO. Pessimists would disagree by saying that "Only when you do something there is a risk of failure. Better don't attempt at all". So should we keep quiet and become passive?

The only people who are branded as failures are the ones who don't even try.

Haven't you heard that the fear of failure is worse than failure itself? Fear of failure shouldn't be the cause for inaction. This fear holds back people from trying once more. Their fears are totally misplaced and unfounded.

Watches may be water-proof but not failure-proof. The same applies to humans as well. None is failure-proof for that matter. Not even successful people. Behind every success there is lot of toil and grind, setbacks and defeats.

Viewing Failures

Failure is only the opportunity to begin again, more intelligently.

—Henry Ford

Our outlook towards failure needs to undergo a radical change. One failure is not the end of all. Nor does it make the guy a failure for the rest of his life. Look at a failure only as a temporary setback. There is nothing to feel ashamed about failing, but putting up with failure is shameful. Understand that it's just an event and not some lacunae in your personality.

Can you face failures without feeling defeated? Failures are part and parcel of our lives. If you can realise this fact, you will be more comfortable in accepting things as they turn out. Your ability to take things in your stride is most important for viewing failures in the proper perspective and deciding the next course of action.

Michael Jordan says, "I have failed over and over again in my life. And that's why I succeed".

Sometimes, failure is a blessing in disguise. It can help you discover your hidden talent, only if you care to look hard enough. One radical viewpoint about failure is this: Failure happens because we are lucky! Take it as another opportunity to face our shortcomings and do something positive about them. All it takes to view defiantly against failure and not to buckle under failure is a small adjustment of our attitude.

Blessed are my mistakes to have made me wiser to recount
All my failures with efforts landed in success!
Only to confirm that 'Failures are the pillars of success'
All my experiences is nothing
But 'Sum total of all my mistakes'

Profit Out of Failure

Acceptance of what has happened is the first step to overcoming the consequences of any misfortune.

—William James

The wise person makes the most of his failure. The fool drops out soon. Failure is life's biggest lesson. It happens when we take things for granted and become irreverent about life. It tempers the unflattering side of our personality from vices like too much ego, pride, arrogance, laziness and indifference.

Failure builds character. It strengthens your resolve and develops fortitude and forbearance. It protects us from becoming overwhelmed by the ups and downs of life.

Failure can be the beginning of many great things to come, if you are tuned to and open to accepting the lessons hidden within.

Failure helps us judge people better. It shows who is who as you get to see people in their true colors and you get the real picture.

When we lose, we must ensure that we don't lose the lesson. Consider failure as a chance to learn and look at things afresh. It is an opportunity for self-introspection. Learning from failures opens up new angles of viewpoint hitherto unknown and makes us wiser in our subsequent attempts. All along we have been talking about failures. Now what is success? Success is failure turned inside out.

Make most of the failure that has befallen you.

Make a New Beginning

Our greatest glory is not in never failing, but in rising every time we fall.

—Confucius

Falling down doesn't matter nearly as much as getting up and trying again. Failure teaches you more than success. Failures are stepping stones to success. When you lose, neither lose your heart nor the lessons.

Never say die. Step after step the ladder is ascended. If at first you don't succeed, try, try, try again!

The period between failure and success is defining. Do something meaningful and avoid squandering time in self-pity or wasteful activities. The most destructive habit is worry. Kick it hard on its face and get on with life.

Brooding over failure will not help; what is essential is to get up and do something, some conscious and determined action towards achieving success. Almost nothing was ever accomplished without setback after setback. Victory tends to go to the resilient. Determination, resolve and relentless efforts are the key ingredients while attempting again.

A failure is still a failure even if you downplay it by keeping up appearances and putting up a brave face. The best anti-dote to failure is success. Make a new beginning today. Start working towards achieving success.

Failures must be a springboard for improvement rather than becoming a net that traps and grounds us. Failures aren't here to bog us down in quick sands.

Failures teach us one thing: Someone rightly said, "Our determination to succeed wasn't enough". When you understand this you will double your efforts towards success.

Only the weak-hearted chicken out. The strong ones renew their dream, strengthen their resolve and go ahead on the face of odds relentlessly and finally succeed.

Failure is Never Final

It's not over until it's over.

—Yogi Berra

Failure is never final — unless you make it one. Trying again is nothing but triumph of hope over experience. Nothing lasts forever — not even your troubles. You are never a loser until you quit trying. Quitting is a permanent solution to a temporary problem. Failures are temporary and they aren't going to stay with you as long as you are going to attempt again. It is one more stone in your path that needs to be turned over.

The logical end of every endeavor is success. Nothing should stop you from achieving your goals. See that you hang on doggedly till the end...to win!

What matters most is belief and faith in ourselves. Renewal of our confidence in ourselves, our skills and abilities is the need of the hour.

War is never lost in the battlefield
But war is finally lost when the commanding self fails in his courage
To carry on the war to victory.
You have not lost so long you are fighting!
Remember, every fall is, but a rise
To know this, is to be wise
As it is no credit, that you never had a fall

But the 'wonder of wonder' is every time you had a fall
You got up again & again!
Winners never quit.
Quitters never win!
Now you will agree that failure is never final!

FAILURES

'Tis better to have tried in vain,
Sincerely striving for a goal,
Than to have lived upon the plain
An idle and a timid soul.

'Tis better to have fought and spent
Your courage, missing all applause,
Than to have in smug content
And never ventured for a cause.

For he who tries and fails may be
The founder of a better day;
Though he never had his victory,
From him shall others learn the way.

—Edgar A. Guest

The Winning Edge

Impossible? That word is not in my dictionary.

—Napoleon Bonaparte

If you look at winners you will find in them the makings of a winner. How? It is not that they become winners overnight. It takes qualities like hard work, patience, perseverance to win. Having the winning edge helps one in overtaking others in the race to win.

The Ingredients of Success

In the search for the makings of success people say 'nowhere' but it is 'now here' within us.

Thoughts + Beliefs + Dream and Vision + Will + Efforts = Success

That's the way success is evolved. Break down self-limiting boundaries that bound you — your thoughts, your vision, your goals. There are simply no limits for you.

Thoughts

Our life is what our thoughts make it.

—Marcus Aurelius

Thoughts are fundamental. Think success. Look success in the eye. As told by Duncan Goodhow, Success is the systematic destruction of failure. Thinking success involves thinking positive. The power of positive thinking is immense. Positive thoughts prompt positive actions that give you positive results.

With positive thoughts you can change your very course of life! Read the following the process that is set in motion by our thoughts.

Good thoughts can change your life

When you can change your thinking
You can change your beliefs.

When you can change your beliefs
You can change your expectations

When you can change your expectations
You can change your attitude

When you can change your attitude
You can change your behavior

When you can change your behavior
You can change your performance

When you can change your performance
You can change your life.

—Anon

Beliefs

To accomplish great things, we must not only act, but also dream; not only plan, but also believe.

—Anatole France

Beliefs are vital. To start with, first believe in yourself — your abilities, talents and skills. We have to believe in the wishes and the belief will strengthen our desire to achieve what we covet. Mere wishes are silly fishes. When we believe our cause, we will leave no stone unturned in our endeavor towards success.

In most people negative factors dominate and shape their beliefs. Ask them to attempt, pat comes their response:

- I cannot do that.
- I am not cut out for that.
- It is too tough for me, etc.

Turn around the corner by leveraging on your strengths. Your strengths and past accomplishments give you the necessary boost to believe in yourself.

Dreams and Vision

Walt Disney said, "If you can 'dream it' you can do it". You visualise the scenario and it becomes a dream. It strengthens our desires. Dreams propel us towards developing the will to succeed. Dreaming big will lead you to achieving big.

So dreams and visions must be big enough in order to achieve big. Build on your dreams.

The Will to Win

> *If you have the will to win, you have achieved half your success; if you don't, you have achieved half your failure.*
>
> —David Ambrose

Everything starts with the will. Where there is a will, there's a way. Nothing is easy to the unwilling. Nothing is impossible to a willing heart. The will-power gets you started, drives you and stops when you win.

"Strength does not come from physical capacity. It comes from an indomitable will" said Jawaharlal Nehru.

Put in your efforts with utmost sincerity for nothing is impossible to a willing heart. Determination is vital to accomplish anything. Once a young man who aspired to study law wrote to Lincoln for advice and Lincoln replied,

> "If you are resolutely determined to make a lawyer of yourself, the thing is more than half done already.... Always bear in mind that your own resolution to succeed is more important than any other one thing".

"Perhaps there is no more important component of character than steadfast resolution. The boy who is going to make a great man, or is going to count in any way in afterlife, must make up in his mind not merely to overcome a thousand obstacles, but to win inspite of a thousand repulses and defeats".

—Theodore Roosevelt

The ability to bounce back when you are hit hard is essential. Harder the hit, higher the bounce just like a tennis ball. Winners are made up of that stuff.

Have the killing spirit to accomplish your goals, despite the odds stacked against you. The person with the killing spirit, fire-in-the-belly will not stop at anything. Simply no excuses he will accept. He will settle for nothing except the achievement of his goals. You get anywhere near having the winning edge if you have the guts to start over again when everything seems hopeless and the horizon is black. Winners have the determination to carry on, come what may, in the face of obstacles towards achieving their goals.

Sir Isaac Newton one of the world's greatest scientists of all time, worked several hours everyday for twenty years and wrote down the brilliant results of his research work in a set of papers. It so happened that one day when he was away his pet dog named Diamond jumped on the table playfully upsetting the burning candle. The bundle of manuscripts caught fire. Twenty years of hard research went up in smoking leaving smoldering ashes. Any other person would have beaten the dog to death black and blue. Newton took it in a cool way and he simply stroked the dog's head and said looking at it with pity, "Oh Diamond, you know not what you have done!"

He once again set about writing. It took him several more years to complete the task. How great were his qualities — the compassion for the dumb animal! The patience and forbearance he displayed! And the guts to start over again when everything was reduced to ashes! Indeed, Newton was as great at heart as in intellect.

Efforts

The will to win is not nearly as important as the will to prepare to win.

—Bobby Knight

The problem most people face is they "desire without deserving". Mere will is no skill. He who wills the end, wills the means. The means are the efforts with which we are going to arrive at the destination. Winning starts with beginning of efforts. Without efforts on our part nothing happens, nothing ever moves at all. Efforts are conscious exertions on our part towards the achievement of success. Our efforts will be meaningful if they are result-oriented. It involves some visible action on ground.

Abraham Lincoln rightly said, "Give me six hours to chop down a tree and I will spend the first four sharpening the axe". Result-oriented efforts involve staying determined till the end. You will not back out at the whiff of first opposition. This makes me to recall the story of a young farmer who kept digging wells in his field. After a few feet of digging he felt dejected at not finding any water. He abandoned the ditch and started digging in a new place. The same thing happened after a few feet and he went to dig 5 different wells in vain. A scholar who passed by saw his activities and advised him to concentrate and focus his energies in one particular spot and from there will spring the most-sought-after water. Thereafter farmer complied and succeeded at last.

So understand that mere will to win is worthless if you do not have the will to prepare. Do you have the resolve to see through until you see the light at the end of the tunnel?

Failure is neither the will nor the fate of a strong person. Winning is a matter of deliberate choice; not chance. Have the guts to carry on even when obstacles confront you on your way. You are bound to win, sooner or later. Every one wants to win. Only those with the winning edge will succeed. Be buoyant and keep winning. Be a winner. You are born to win!

THERE IS NOTHING YOU CANNOT DO!

There is nothing to fear —
You're as good as the best,
As strong as the mightiest, too.
You can win in every battle or test;
For there's no one just like you.

There's only one you in the world today;
So nobody else, you see.
Can do your work in as fine a way;
You're the only you there'll be!

So face the world, and all life is yours
To conquer and love and live;
And you'll find the happiness that endures
In just the measure you give;

There's nothing too good for you to possess.
Nor heights where you cannot go;
Your power is more than belief or guess —
It is something you have to know.

There is nothing to fear — you can and you will.
For you're the invincible you.
Set your foot on the highest hill —
There's nothing you cannot do.

—Author Unknown

Attitude is Everything

Attitude is the first quality that marks the successful man. If he has a positive attitude and is a positive thinker, who likes challenges and difficult situations, then he has half his success achieved.

—Lowell Peacock

Sporting the right attitude before starting any endeavor is critical. The process of change begins with us. It starts with the change in our attitudes. Your attitude constitutes how well you are mentally disposed towards perceiving things.

Attitude Measures Your Altitude

The only disability in life is a bad attitude.

—Scott Hamilton

Your attitude performs a crucial function. It can act either as a deciding factor or a limiting factor. There is nothing more debilitating for improvement than negative attitude.

Most executives suffer from attitude problems. Align your attitude that is in line with your organisation's goals and objectives. That way you stay on the right and winning side.

"If It's to Be, It's Upto Me"

Let us not follow where the path may lead.
Let us go instead where there's no path and leave a trail.

—Japanese proverb

You can complain because roses have thorns, or you can rejoice because thorns have roses. Or you can see a half-filled cup and say it is half-empty or half-full. It's all upto you how you look at things. Attitude is all that matters. Perception is shaped by the attitude we have and it is the deciding factor — whether you approve or disapprove, start ahead or stay behind. Ages ago Hannibal said:

"We will either find a way or make one".

Ego-centric to Geo-centric

Ego is the biggest threat or impediment towards having the right attitude. The following attitudes must be avoided at all costs:

- I-Me-Myself
- I-know-it-all
- I am-better-than-you
- I-don't-care-what-happens-to-you

These attitudes reflect the egotistic tendencies and selfish motives in us. Superiority complex plays the spoilsport in contributing towards building an egoistic attitude which exudes negativity and excludes others. Change yourself from being 'ego-centric to geo-centric' personality.

Right Attitude Spells Success

Nothing can stop the man with right mental attitude from achieving his goal; nothing on earth can help the man with the wrong mental attitude.

—W.W. Ziege

You are only an attitude away from success. Attitudinal change or rather the willingness on one's part to change attitude is important to move towards the right direction.

Positive thoughts constitute right attitude. Negativity has no place when you have the right attitude. Losers say "Nowhere". Winners say "Now here". Before you say "I can't", say "I will try" and do your best.

Attitude determines how much of the future we are allowed to see. It acts as the deciding factor of our dreams and visions and it influences our determination and resolve when we are confronted with challenges.

Your attitude defines your outlook. One may see a situation as a problem while another may look at it as a challenge or rather an opportunity to take on a challenge. It's all in the mind and it is the attitude which perceives things as they appear.

Attitude Towards Work

The test of a vocation is the love of the drudgery it involves.

—Unknown

For most of us, our attitude to work needs an honest re-look. Often we feel we haven't got the right break and grumble that we have been given a raw deal. However, all it takes to settle our misgivings is just a small adjustment in our attitudes. Let me illustrate this with how we can effect a change in the way we view our work:

> Two men met in a bus and started talking. "What do you do for a living?" asked one.
>
> "I stamp letters at the post office".
>
> "That must be a boring job".
>
> "Boring? Never! We get to stamp a different date every day!"

It's just a matter of how one views work. It all depends on the perspective with which you look at things. That defines the attitude towards your work as well.

Does your attitude radiate supreme confidence at work? Ready to take on the challenges? Finally remember,

"Outlook determines outcome
Attitude determines action"

Our attitude is an asset, a priceless treasure which must be protected from external negative influences. Possessing the right attitude is one of the requisites of successful personalities. Nurture the right attitude — positive attitude because attitude really is everything!

FORMULA FOR SUCCESS!!!

A small truth to make our life 100% successful

IF

A B C D E F G H I J K L M 1 2 3 4 5 6 7 8 9 10 11 12 13 14 15
N O P Q R S T U V W X Y Z Is equal to 16 17 18 19 20 21 22 23 24 25 26

Then :

H+A+R+D+W+O+R+K = 8+1+18+4+23+15+18+11 = 98%

K+N+O+W+L+E+D+G+E = 11+14+15+23+12+5+4+7+5 = 96%

L + O + V + E = 12+15+22+5 = 54%

L + U + C + K = 12+21+3+11 = 47%

None of them makes 100%!!!!

....

Then what makes 100% ???

Is it Money? ..... No!!!!!

Leadership? ...... No!!!!

Every problem has a solution, only if we perhaps change our

"A T T I T U D E".

It is OUR ATTITUDE towards Life and Work that makes OUR Life 100%

Successful...

A+T+T+I+T+U+D+E = 1+20+20+9+20+21+4+5 = 100%

—Anon

Belief in Oneself

Your chances of success in any undertaking can always be measured by your belief in yourself.

—Robert Collier

The greatest asset one can have is faith. Rock-strong faith that you can move mountains. Without faith you will fail.

Self is Supreme

Everything starts with the self. If you set your heart on something and are determined to do it no one, no force on earth can stop you from your endeavor. On the other hand, if you don't want to do something and even if hundred persons urge you to go ahead you will not move forward a step. So self is supreme.

Principles of a Strong Personality

Self-observation

Keenly observe yourself. Detach and see your conduct and activities. Be a witness. As an outsider you will be able to view more of yourself, where you go wrong and what is the right course of action.

Self-observation is being conscious about oneself. You evaluate yourself and start using your discriminating power. With discretion you will be able to make proper judgments and better decisions. Be self-observant.

Self-reliance

If you want to get ahead you will have to learn to stand on your own legs. Expecting others to do your job or do something on behalf of you will not help. Find ways and means to be self-made. A successful person firmly believes in the saying, "Self-help is the best help" and gets going without waiting for anyone.

Depending on others will make you dependant even for small tasks. You will not move forward and you will be dictated by the people you are dependant upon. You are self-contained person. So be self-reliant.

Self-responsible

To be self-responsible means the ability to take full ownership and accountability to your actions. That way you will learn to face the harsh realities better. When you realise that you are the architect of your own life you will appreciate in taking charge of yourself and owning up your actions.

Being self-responsible gives you credibility and you are valued by people. Reliability and trustworthiness become the hallmark of your personality. You are viewed as a man of your words and man of substance. Be self-responsible.

Self-initiative

Doing on your own accord without being told by others is being self-initiated. Being self-directed means you know what you are doing and that you are doing for the right reason. Self-directed persons achieve a lot more than others. Others needn't have to be on your back to get you going. Be a self-starter. Be self-driven.

Self-exertion

If mountain doesn't go to Mohammed, Mohammed must go to the mountain. Self-exertion means being ready to work your way towards the top. You don't merely wish or day-dream for someone to do your job. You are prepared to put in the hard work it takes to make your dreams come true.

You are also determined to exert yourself towards your goals. Lethargy and procrastination has no place in your mind. Be self-exerted.

Self-resolution

You don't settle for anything less than the best. You are self-propelled in your determination and resolve. You go according to your convictions and beliefs. The steely resolve comes from the quest for achievement and to carve a niche for oneself. Be self-resolved.

Self-dignity

You are a self-respecting individual. You possess a proper sense of your own dignity and integrity. A person with self-dignity would break in defiance rather bend in compromise. He is dignity-personified. He would rather forego his need and maintain his dignity.

The values and principles you cherish will not permit you to go below a level or stoop down to gain a favor or advantage. You know your self-worth and act accordingly. Be self-dignified.

Self-esteem for Self-confidence

Self-confidence is the first requisite to great undertakings

—Samuel Johnson

One of the most priceless possessions in life an individual can have is self-esteem. Self-esteem is the way we feel about ourselves. Our mood swings often determine how we esteem ourselves — high or low. High self-esteem breeds self-confidence and low self-esteem makes us to feel down all the time.

It is pertinent to have high self-esteem of ourselves. To develop high self-esteem we must form the habit of valuing ourselves, our potential and our worth.

Many people confuse self-esteem with happiness. Mere happiness cannot ensure self-esteem while self-esteem can bring happiness and confidence. After all, self-esteem is all about feeling our worth and rating our self-worth.

Self-confidence is closely associated with self-esteem. A person with high self-esteem will have abundant self-confidence. Self-confidence is the boon; over-confidence is the bane. Self-confidence stems from positive self-image, self-esteem and beliefs in one's abilities. Over-confidence springs from mastery, expertise, familiarity or past successes. Be on your guard against over-confidence from rearing its ugly head and play the spoilsport.

The key ingredient to success is self-confidence. This is one quality which is essential to your personal and professional growth.

You don't have to be anyone else but you. Inside you there is a force more powerful than all the hype in the world. CONFIDENCE. You have got it. Confidence in yourself is enough to take on the world.

Competence gives confidence. Confidence needn't necessarily have to be expressed in an extrovert way. Let self-consciousness give way for self-confidence. Be self-confident. Remember, you will get nowhere unless you have tremendous self-confidence — faith in yourself!

Believe in yourself — your abilities, your skills and talents. Step out into the world with supreme confidence. Self-confidence spurred ordinary people to great undertakings, find success that made them successful. If they can, you can too! Just believe in yourself!

BELIEVE IN YOURSELF

There may be days when you get up in the morning and
things aren't the way you had hoped they would be,
....that's when you have to tell yourself that things
will get better.

There are times when people disappoint you and let you down,
but those are the times when you must remind yourself to
trust your own judgments and opinions, to keep your life
focused on believing in yourself and all that you are
capable of.

There will be challenges to face and changes to make in
your life,
and it is up to you to accept them.

Constantly keep yourself headed in the right direction for
you. It may not be easy at times, but in those times of
struggle you will find a stronger sense of who you are, So
when the days come that are filled with frustration
and unexpected responsibilities.

Remember to believe in yourself and all you want your
life to be, because the challenges and changes will
only help you to find the goals that you know are
meant to come true for you.

Keep believing in yourself.

—Author Unknown

Image-building — Your Personal Brand Identity

Image is like reputation: difficult to earn, easy to lose and extremely hard to regain.

First impressions are often lasting ones. The image we project plays a crucial role in the way others perceive us. And our personalities reveal more about our image.

Personality transcends beyond mundane things like your name, profession, lineage and other external identities. Your personality, the Collins dictionary states, is the sum total of all the behavioral and mental characteristics by means of which you are recognised as being unique.

So to make your personality stand out distinctly you must develop it through image-building — your personal brand identity.

Building Your Self-image

You cannot consistently perform in a manner which is inconsistent with the way you see yourself.

—R. Joyce Brothers

Outward image is what most people are concerned about. Good. No denying. They do matter. More than all the cosmetics that help you to keep up appearances what counts is your ability to exude confidence and cheerfulness. That starts with a simple smile. Keep smiling. A smile doesn't cost anything and pays big dividends. Not only does it make you feel good, but it makes everyone else feel better too. It spreads the feel-good factor around.

When you come across someone be the first to say, "Hello! Glad to see you". It exudes cheerfulness, openness and a delight in meeting people. Furthermore, it projects you as a person who values people rather than ignoring their presence altogether.

The first step towards building your image is taking care of your self-image. Your self-image could be negative or positive. If it is positive build on it. If it is negative take steps to transform it into a positive one.

There is nothing more demeaning than having a negative self-image of oneself. One reason for this negativity is due to the feeling of inadequacy of ourselves, our potential and the ever-elusive success. Our experiences have made us to believe we are mediocre, incapable of doing anything worthwhile or hitting it big out of life. This mentality has just got psyched into our being and we have come to believe we are like that.

If someone asks you, "What do you say if this year you are getting a double promotion? Or you are selected for

'Best Employee Award?'" Most of us have this attitude about our own image, "Me? No chance". This negativity is entrenched strong and deep in our psyches.

Very few have got a self-image of themselves good enough to say, "Yes. Perhaps, I deserve" or "Why not?"

The development of a positive self-image is contributed, as we will see one after another, by our behavior, manners, gestures, habits, attitude (perception), temperament amongst others. All these emanate from the self-awareness of your identity and potential differentiating you from others.

Behavior

Behavior is a mirror in which every one displays his image.

—Goethe

At heart of right behavior is the concern for others and sensitiveness, their feelings. Right behavior implies being courteous and polite — always. After all, life is not too short to be courteous. Let your relationships with people be marked by cordiality and consideration.

Common sense is very uncommon. Having a common sense approach while dealing with people is necessary for successful projection of the right image. It involves displaying a superior degree of maturity in behavior as well.

A gentleman isn't complete without proper behavior.

Manners

Manners are what vex or soothe, corrupt or purify, exalt or debase, barbarize or refine us, by a contrast, uniform, insensible operation, like that of the air we breath in.

—Edmund Burke

Good manners are the blossoms of good sense and good feelings.

—M.A. Kelly

Personal grooming alone isn't enough to charm your way. Manners matter much. A well-groomed person with impeccable manners will be welcome everywhere.

Manners could be as basic as these. Never ask for anything from anybody. And on the other way round, if anyone asks for something never say no. It's not manners to refuse when someone asks for it specifically. And when you give something forget about it forever. Neither remind about it nor ask for it again.

Extending little courtesies like asking for permission before smoking go a long way in portraying you as a person of good manners.

However to ask for help when you cannot do without and to accept help isn't bad. People with good manners have common sense in abundance.

Gestures

Small kindness, small courtesies, small considerations, habitually practiced in our social contacts, give a great charm to the character than the display of great talents and accomplishments.

—M.A. Kelly

Little gestures on your part — whoever you are, however high may be the position you may hold — go a long way in enhancing your image. A comforting word, a warm smile, a pat in the back, walking till the threshold while seeing off someone could mean a lot to people. Good gestures at the right time will earn you goodwill and support.

Habits

Make good habits and they will make you.

—Anon

Habits are for life. They are formed early in our lives and stay on with us shaping our manners and behavior. Good habits reflect our upbringing, social class, grooming and our caliber. They affect the people with whom we deal in our day-to-day lives.

Peter Amsterdam says how habits are formed with an interesting anecdote:

Believe it or not, they used to build bridges by first flying a kite from one side of the river to the other. Someone on the opposite side caught the kite and tied a little thicker, stronger string to the end of the kite string, and the men who had sent the kite over pulled the new, thicker string back across. The teams on each side kept repeating the process, next with an even stronger string, then a cord, then a thin rope, and so on. Eventually they could pull a small steel cable across, then a heavier one, until finally they had a cable across the expanse that was strong enough to support them and their tools and materials. And it all started with one tiny kite string!

That's how habits are formed, both good and bad. Add a thread every day, and before long you can't break it. Start developing a good habit by taking the first step, however small, in the right direction. Then keep at it until you've built up a routine that can't easily be broken.

Perception

We judge ourselves by what we feel capable of doing, while others judge us by what we have already done. Your attitude plays a vital role in perceiving things. Having a positive attitude towards the world at large is essential to look at things in the right perspective. You can either say the glass if half-full or half-empty. It depends on how you look at it.

Temperament

Are you cool or snappy? Ideally, everyone aspiring to sport a positive self-image must have a sweet temperament that is characterized by patience, concern for others and by being genial to one and all you come across in your course of life — at work and beyond.

Personal Brand Identity

Building yourself a personal brand identity gives you a unique and distinct image setting you apart from others.

Mere academic degrees or job competence isn't enough anymore. To stand tall and get counted in a workplace consisting of best of the breed, personal branding is an essential component for exhibiting your personality. It shows you in the right picture and establishes you as a person who is a cut above the rest

The benefits of having your own personal brand identity are immense. They are intangible and you will feel the returns as you exploit your potential to the optimum and gain more out of life.

However, let's get it right with a few facts about creating a personal brand identity. It is not about sporting a different image to the outside world and remaining just the same inside. In the process of building your brand identity, you understand your traits and attributes which are unique to all of us — strengths, abilities, skills, talents, values, drives and passions. The effectiveness of your personal brand identity revolves around these and utilising them to differentiate yourself and guide your way successfully towards not just in your professional lives but also enriching your personal lives.

Building your personal brand identity happens in the following ways:

1. Rediscover your personality
2. Redefine your personality
3. Reinvent your personality

REDISCOVER YOUR PERSONALITY

Know Yourself

The weaver knows best where his net is weak or strong. You are the right person to know yourself the best. Calm self-introspection will bring out the hidden strengths and help you know your true potential. Everyone is endowed with some skills and talents which many think too small to matter. To many it doesn't mean much. But that makes a crucial difference to your life — success or failure.

Focus on your strengths but be aware of your weaknesses too. Know what drives you, what you stand for and what you are looking for.

When you know and gauge your real potential, your self-image takes a decisive turn for the better. The ensuing revelation sets in motion a chain reaction. Your self-worth increases which in turn serves as a morale-booster that gives you a high self-esteem of yourself. With a high self-esteem guess what you have? Self-confidence, right attitude and finally a positive self-image!

Be Yourself

Be yourself. The world worships the original.

—Ingrid Bergman

Behave naturally whoever you are with, wherever you are. Be a first-rate version of yourself, than a second-rate version of someone else. Observe others and learn but don't imitate. In your bid to build up your personality avoid copying. You cannot build a positive self-image by impersonating someone for long. You cannot be what you are apparently not. While an original is always rare to see but it is easy to recognise. Be yourself. Be an original.

REDEFINE YOUR PERSONALITY

Shape up

Shaping up is a vital process in re-defining your personality. It is a conscious and deliberate effort to better yourself. Kick off old habits particularly the bad ones. Plug the loopholes and flaws in your character. For instance, if you are a habitual liar, vow yourself not to lie henceforth. Correct yourself the various anomalies that plague your personality. Simple efforts aimed at setting the record straight make a lot of difference to your personality.

Refine Yourself

While refining yourself you improvise, filter, distill, polish all those things for which you stand for. Out of these come finesse and elegance. Gruffness and roughness give way for smoothness. Refining yourself is shaping yourself so as to provide that finishing touch as opposed to rawness. Knowing your potential you re-orient your goals and ambitions. You just get better all the while.

REINVENT YOUR PERSONALITY

Re-make Yourself

The first step in re-inventing your personality starts with re-making yourself. Take a complete break from the past. Don't suffer from hangovers. To re-make yourself you need to start afresh. But build on your past successes and the present strengths and other traits you possess.

Re-fashion Yourself

You will have to strengthen the resolve to get an absolutely brand new image for yourself. It starts with the change process and how determined you are in your endeavor to re-fashion your image. By re-fashioning I don't mean a cosmetic facelift but a real change, tangible change in your personality.

Emulate worthy people whom you may come across — at work it could be successful professionals who made it to the top, or charismatic people who do good things in the society at large.

You can claim to have re-invented your personality only when it undergoes a complete revamp for the better. You rise above the herd and get noticed.

The merits of your personal brand identity are intangible. They help you in:

1. Defining your core personality.
2. Channelising your personal energy in a positive and constructive way.
3. Enhancing your personal charisma.
4. Boosting your confidence levels.
5. Increasing your visibility and presence.
6. Displaying yourself as someone distinctly different from others.
7. Gaining respect from others.

The entire personal branding exercise analyses you part by part, trait by trait and makes you to realise that you as an individual in the corporate machine is a class apart.

Your personal brand identity is critical to achieving your goals and letting the world know what you are standing for — your values, principles and philosophy. It helps in projecting your self-image in such a manner that people tend to perceive you as someone whose personality is at its best and different from the rest.

And finally, the aim of your personal brand identity is to exude confidence, cheerfulness, poise and the will to take on anything that comes on your way. Everything is optimism-personified about you. You gain a charisma of your own.

Now think for yourself. What's the impression your personality is giving when you meet people? What's the personal statement you are making? What's the message you are sending across? Re-fashion your image. Re-invent your personality. Get out of the pile by leveraging on your personal brand identity and get a new image!

6

TIME MANAGEMENT

Time your time well

- Today is My Time
- The Value of Time

It has been my observation that most people get ahead during the time that others waste.

—Henry Ford

It is one universal fact that the only difference between two individuals is not how much time they have — because we all have 24 hours in a day — but how that time is used. Time is one commodity that is given in same quantity for every one of us.

First understand that time cannot be managed. It is we who have to manage ourselves according to the eternal flow called 'Time'. Time is, simply, uncontrollable.

Many people, particularly business executives, complain that they don't have time. They seem to be perpetually in a race with time to finish their job. But it is the successful man who has got time for everything because he has mastered the art of time management. Just bear in mind for sure that the guy who says he doesn't have time for something because he is 'busy' is one who just doesn't know how to effectively use time. A busy man always has time to do everything. Availability of time is as simple as this: if you don't find time during day, steal it from night!

Time and Tide Wait for None

Time flies. To avoid wondering where all the time has gone follow the words of Lord Chesterfield,

> "I recommend to you to take care of the minutes; for the hours will take care of themselves".

According to Horace Mann,

> "Lost, yesterday. Somewhere between sunrise and sunset, two golden hours, each with sixty diamond minutes. No reward is offered, for they are gone forever".

The First Step

The first step in time-management starts with you. To start with be punctual always. Someone has defined that *punctuality is the first simple test of a sense of duty, discipline, devotion and honesty.* Become famous for being punctual for every meeting or appointment you keep.

Punctuality is one aspect which never gets out-of-fashion or old fashioned. It always has its own value and people who are punctual mean business and they are serious. Avoid wasting other's time by arriving late and making excuses. Just as how important your time is to you the same is for others. Remember that the real efficacy of punctuality lies in its consistency. And above all, punctuality reflects your image, caliber and how serious are you in valuing your time.

In Time or On time?

Be in time rather than on time. A person who is in time is a good planner. On the other hand, a person who is on time is not so. There always exist an element of risk and subsequent tension in being on time.

As such, on time is good but in time is better!

When you begin to manage your time well, you will realize that you suffer less from stress. Most executives don't plan their day in advance. Lack of organising things is the bane from which people suffer. A well-organised and scheduled day will be smooth sailing for the busy executive to complete all his assigned tasks within the deadline.

TIPS FOR TIME MANAGEMENT

When Thomas Edison was asked what the most important item in the world was, he answered, "Time". So understand that lost time can never be got back.

The following ten tips will help you in better time management:

1. Plan Your Day in Advance

Effective time management starts with good planning. Have a game plan for the day. Time your time well. Plan the work, work the plan. It is as simple as that.

Charles C. Gibbons says,

"One of the best ways to save time is to think and plan ahead; five minutes of thinking can often save an hour of work".

Planning is of two types:

1. Short-term
2. Long-term

Here, understand that despite all your planning be it short-term or long-term, action lies in the short-term with a vision on the long-term.

For some it is always rush hour and they get confused and tensed doing up their work at the eleventh hour. It happens every time in the face of looming deadlines. The malaise is in improper or no planning at all.

List out the things that you have to do the next day before you take your dinner. Better still if you can put them down in writing. Use a planner. You will have a clear idea as to what your tasks are and how you will go about doing them. Simply put, planning gives the edge of accomplishing maximum with minimum time.

2. Organise Your Work Desk

It has been found that people who have cluttered work desk waste lot of time in searching for papers, memos, pens and other miscellaneous items. Keep your telephone, pens, papers and other frequently used items handy.

Your work desk reflects your image. It lets people to know your concern and how well you care for your work. People can easily find out what kind of person you are, your caliber and capabilities just by glancing at your work desk. Moreover, a neatly organised, clean and tidy and well-arranged work place has a soothing effect on your mind and it spurs you to perform your job better. And most importantly, it's the first step towards efficiency.

3. Homework Helps You

Do your homework well before attending meetings and presentations. Research about the topic you are going to present, know the meeting's agenda before hand. Get the facts and figures and go through them. Adequate preparation will save immense time later and possibly from goof-ups too.

4. Think Today not Tomorrow

Resolve to do today what you want to do tomorrow. This way you can avoid procrastination. Whatever you want to do 'Just Do It Now'. Set about doing things at once. Make it a practice until it becomes a habit. Postponing things will land you in more trouble and stress.

In the words of Oprah Winfrey, "Doing the best at this moment puts you in the best place for the next moment".

Avoid procrastination at all costs. Procrastination has been biggest culprit in plans going haywire. As it is said about procrastination it steals away time. It is a deadly habit which will play havoc on a person's effectiveness. A successful executive can ill-afford to procrastinate.

Ralph Waldo Emerson opines,

> "Every day is the best of all. One of the illusions of life is that the present hour is not the critical, decisive hour. Write it on your heart that everyday is the best day of the year".

Do-it-right-now or DIRN in management parlance, is the antidote to procrastination. Never put off until tomorrow what you can manage to wriggle out of today. Start here and now.

Do not postpone the unpleasant and difficult tasks. Do them now, and you will feel much better afterwards. Or simply, nurture that 'Just-do-it-now' attitude.

5. No Interruptions Please!

Keep your prime working hours free from interruptions. Let everyone know that you shouldn't be disturbed during particular hours of the day. You save lot of time when you are left in peace to do your job. Be alert of people who waste your time and learn to say 'no' to them.

However, in your bid to have interruption-free productivity time, don't shut out yourself from others. Schedule free-time so that others have chance to speak, communicate and clarify things with you.

6. Prioritise Your Tasks

List out the tasks on basis of their priority and rank them on a scale of 1 to 10 classifying them as the most important to least important. Use "Things to do list" pads for effectiveness.

Prioritising helps in completing the job ahead of schedule without compromising on the quality of the work done. A job undertaken in a calm and composed manner will turn out well as opposed to one that is finished in a slip-shod manner in the face of looming deadline.

Don't let your list to overwhelm you. Set about doing and as and when you finish cross out the task. Rewrite the prioritized tasks every day afresh.

The trouble is not everyone is adept in prioritising their tasks. In the words of French philosopher Blaise Pascal,

"The last thing one knows is what to put first".

In effect, most people go about doing their work according to the pressure they are subjected to rather than the priorities they have.

Whether in life or in work, what is vital for success is your ability to get your priorities right.

Time Management Matrix

Time Management Matrix is one popular method talked about in any time discussion on time management. See the following diagram and choose which task number you perform normally in your work schedule.

Time Management Matrix

Task # 1 **Very Urgent and Important**	Task # 2 **Urgent but not Important**
Task # 3 **Not Urgent but Important**	Task # 4 **Not Urgent and not Important**

Normally, people choose Task # 1 'Very Urgent and Important'. However, one must think how things have come to such a pass that Task # 1 tops the priority list. Instead, a successful and systematic executive will always concentrate on Task # 4 'Not Urgent and Not Important'. When Task # 4 is done in a time-bound result-oriented manner, we don't have to face any other tasks. So focus on Task # 4 and other task situations don't have a chance to arise at all!

One universal truth is that any work is important but not always urgent. They come under Task # 3. Procrastination makes the work to progress from Task # 3 to Task # 1 crying for immediate attention. Any work in Task # 1 never waits. It gets done but with the result that the quality of the work comes down which could have been avoided if the work had been completed in Task # 3 itself.

Suppose you have to submit a report detailing the sales forecast for the next five years within two weeks to your boss. The first thought in which we get comfort is "Still two weeks are there. I have plenty of time". We tend to reserve our attention to a later day. Even before we can take note of, time flies in a jiffy. The deadline looms large ahead and the work remains unfinished. You cut a sorry figure on the D-Day which you could have avoided.

The best strategy to utilise the time optimally and finish our tasks well ahead is to complete the tasks in the short-term with pain, toil and grind and this will become long-term pleasure.

Finally it all boils down to as simple as this: "Do not postpone the unpleasant and difficult tasks. Do them now, and you will feel much better afterwards. Do important jobs *now* before they become urgent".

7. Adopt 'Open the bundle approach'

The man who removes a mountain begins by carrying away small stones.

—Chinese proverb

On the face of it, every major task will look daunting and overwhelming. People quit or try to postpone or at least try to ignore the task. Postponing or ignoring will not help as sooner or later you will have to finish the job. One way to tackle them is to break them into manageable chunks — tasks that can be done in a short time. If you are asked to break a bundle of logs at one go you cannot do it. But when you open the bundle and take out the sticks one by one you can easily break them. The same applies to your day-to-day tasks. This way you save time and energy. What was once considered difficult becomes easy and achievable.

8. Delegate to Deliver the Goods in Time, Every Time

One effective way to utilise your time is to delegate work. Delegation helps in accomplishing things when time is scarce. What one man can do, two or more can do better and that too in short time. When you learn to effectively delegate to others, and empower them to succeed everyone wins. If you are smart enough to get things done through others you are winning this race with time.

9. Use Technology to Aid in Your Work

All the technology available in the world is here to enable us to perform better in our jobs. See technology as an aid to your work and not as a hindrance. Invest your time in learning to use common technology devices and mediums like the telephone, mobile phone, pager, e-mail, fax, etc. Small conveniences like pre-programming your telephone with frequently called numbers, fixing auto-dialer and hands-free speaker phones, learning short cut keys while operating computer, getting it right with the paper size and recipient number when sending fax can save lot of time and loss of productivity. Use appropriate means of communication to get swift responses. Reduce your reliance on others for doing your job like depending on secretaries for typing letters, sub-staff for taking Photostat copies, etc. Learn to use computers, fax machines, Photostat machines yourself. They help in avoiding time delays in business communications.

10. Set a Target Time and Date for Every Task

Finally, any assigned task's accomplishment will be certain to some extent only when you set a target time and date. Without them there is nothing to self-direct and automatically control your time schedule towards performing them.

Seldom have we found some people who have such a regulated life that by their movements you can set the time of your watch! Can you become like them? Or at least regularize and streamline your activities?

If you observe carefully, those who make the worst use of their time complain of its shortness and inadequacy.

TIME MANAGEMENT STRATEGY

The strategy to manage your time and gaining some control over it is adopting the following two policies in your work style:

1. Touch and Go

Our professions demand us to distribute our attention on many things. More often, we find ourselves having a finger on every pie. But the problem is many of us just don't touch and go. We touch and stick on! That grounds us making us unable to do justice to all the jobs that are entrusted to us.

2. Learning to Say 'No'

Learn to say no to time-wasters. Most executives get entangled in things that are not directly connected with their jobs. Later they fret and fume about the lack of time in the face of deadlines looming large. Understand that every moment you waste in preoccupation is a moment you steal from productivity. Streamline your executive lifestyle and avoid getting preoccupied with classic time wasters.

Know about the classic time wasters in your business hours:

1. Telephone interruptions.
2. Crisis Management — fire-fighting always.

3. Lack of clear objectives and goals.
4. Priority to entertain drop-in visitors.
5. Ineffective delegation of work.
6. Attempting to wear too many hats simultaneously.
7. Attending numerous meetings.
8. Cluttered work areas.
9. Inability to say 'no'.
10. Lack of self-discipline.
11. Procrastination.
12. Untrained Staff.
13. Inadequate, inaccurate, unreliable, delayed information.
14. Leaving task unfinished.
15. Lack of clear communication or channels for communication.
16. Confused responsibility and authority.
17. Haste and impatience.
18. Frequent travel that don't serve the purpose.
19. People not available.
20. Lethargy.

But be aware that saying 'no' has serious implications. In the first place, friction will arise. People will get cross with you. But over time people will observe you — your progress, your determination and then will understand that you mean business. They will stop disturbing you.

All said and done, time management is sheer common sense. Nothing hi-fi or it is not a management fad. Just plan and do your job in a time-bound manner. It is a wonderful art to be practiced not only in our job but also in every activity we intend to undertake. No matter how many one-day courses you attend or books you read on time-management you cannot master this art until you take some conscious efforts to bring them as part of your executive life-style.

Our lives are but a journey with time. Alas frequently, we are in race against time. Time spent is life spent. Time wasted is life wasted. Spend your time with value-addition. Time's productivity is life's productivity. A person who is in control of his time is in control of his life. Simply, time management is life management.

Time is a precious commodity, and once spent cannot be replaced. It was Napoleon Bonaparte, who said,

"Ask me for anything but time".

We know well that procrastination is the thief of time. Every moment we waste in preoccupation of our time doing nothing or doing silly things is but the time we steal from productivity. That's the way companies view procrastination of its employees.

With effective time management you can accomplish more within limited time and to the satisfaction of every one concerned. It will improve your personal effectiveness and you will become famous for finishing difficult tasks ahead of time. So become the consummate time manager so as to manage your time well and not to allow time to manage you!

Today is My Time

Which is the best day?

Today!

Every day is the best of all.
One of the illusions of life is that the present hour is not critical, decisive one. Write it on your heart that everyday is the best day of the year.

—Ralph Waldo Emerson

***

Forget the past — for we can never change it.
Forget the future — for we cannot be definite about it.
Think only about the present — for we can change it as we like at every moment.

***

Thinking of yesterday makes us prisoners of the past.
Thinking of tomorrow makes us dreamers.
Thinking of today makes us to live in the present and do something.

***

We can imbibe lessons from the past.
We can dream about the future.

But the real reward comes from the effective and proper utilization of the present.

***

Tomorrow is promised to no one.
Today is what we live
Yesterday is a memory
Forget it and forgive.

Tomorrow may never happen
Today is occurring right now
Yesterday will become a blur
If only we allow.

Tomorrow is only a dream
That may or may not come true
Today is the only day that counts
In the life of me and you.

***

TIME DEPOSIT

If you had a bank that credited your account each morning with Rs. 86,400, that carried over no balance from day-to-day — allowed you to keep no cash in your account — and every evening cancelled whatever part of the amount you had failed to use during the day, what would you do? Draw out every rupee every day, of course, and use it to your advantage!

Well, you have such a bank — and its name is Time. Every morning it credits you with 86,400 seconds. Every night it rules off as lost whatever of this you have failed to invest to good purpose. It carries over no balances. It allows no overdrafts. If you fail to use the days' deposits, the loss is yours. There is no going back. There is no drawing against tomorrow. It is us to each of us to invest this precious fund of hours, minutes and seconds in order to get from it the utmost in health, happiness and success.

—Anonymous

***

"'Yesterday' is gone,
'Today' is in your hands,

'Tomorrow' never comes!
Yesterday is a passed cheque,
Today is the only cash,
Tomorrow is only a promissory note.
'Time' is the richest treasure every one equally has,
So spend it wisely and well!"

—Anon

The Value of Time

To realize the value of ONE YEAR,
Ask a student who failed in grade

To realize the value of ONE MONTH,
Ask a mother who gave birth to a premature baby

To realize the value of ONE WEEK,
Ask an editor whose weekly has the largest circulation

To realize the value of ONE DAY,
Ask a laborer who lost his daily wages.

To realize the value of ONE HOUR,
Ask two lovers waiting for each other.

To realize the value of ONE MINUTE,
Ask a person who missed his train.

To realize the value of ONE SECOND,
Ask a person who just escaped an accident.

To realize the value of ONE MILLISECOND,
Ask a person who won a silver medal in Olympics.

Treasure every moment you live.
And remember that time waits for no one.
The past is history. The future is mystery.
The present is a gift!!!

—Anon

What a wonderful thing a day is!
Nothing is more highly to be prized than the value of each day.

—Goethe

Each of us is given a pocketful of time to spend however we may. We use what we will. We waste what we will. But we can never get back a day.

—Roger Wilcox

7

BE THE IDEAL SUBORDINATE

Playing your part willingly

- Nothing Comes Free
- Thriving in Change
- Four Follies to Avoid

He profits most who serves best

At the outset, understand that every boss was once a subordinate. Today you are under someone; tomorrow you may be the boss. Until then play your role properly and you will find yourself on your way to become the boss. However, in your endeavor there are a few random points to be noted and taken care of:

Just do it!

Sometimes our best is simply not best....
We have to do what is required.

—Sir Winston Churchill

Know that in certain situations, however highly qualified and experienced you may be, however right and sensible may be your stand, the boss is always right. Do it just as he says. I say just do it with no questions asked.

Arguing will only show you in poor light at times and can be perceived as insubordination. Bosses never like their activities or decisions questioned that too by their own subordinates. This happens with bosses who are viewed as insensible.

Be Content

People are still willing to do an honest day's work. The trouble is they want a week's pay for it.

—Joey Adams

Contentment is a way to achieve peace of mind.

Initially all you wanted was job. That was something which you needed badly. Now after some time if you are going to crave for the sun and the moon just because your colleagues got it then you are just heading straight for disaster. It's like the camel taking over the tent. Hope you know the story of how once a camel staggered in to a tent begging the shepherd for a small amount of space just to save its head from the hot sun. Upon being allowed it started slowly to put inside its front legs, then hump, body and its hind legs and finally the boy had to go out of his tiny tent so as to make room for the camel. The camel took over the tent! No company would give such allowances. Get in touch with reality with your foot firmly rooted to the ground. Don't live in a fool's paradise. As the saying goes "When you have a lemon, make a lemonade" instead of craving for apples and grapes.

Comparison with others will shatter your peace of mind. It's a sure way to buy worries. Realise that you are unique and you are beyond compare. That way you will be more happy and at peace with yourself.

Don't slip into mission amnesia. You are on the payroll to work towards achieving organizational goals alone and nothing else.

Do it in Public

Never tell your boss an idea when he is alone. For he would later propose the same and take credit for the initiative. Always do it in public.

After all, your boss is not that bad as you think. He is also a human being just like us. Remember he too was once a subordinate like us before he became boss. The problem with him is his ego, which is a bit bloated. Feeding his ego is the only way to his heart.

Present with Panache

An idea is not worth much until a man is found who has the energy and the ability to make it work.

—Philip Dormer Stanhope

Present your ideas and suggestions with panache. He might shoot down at the first hearing. But you need to have that knack of presenting. As someone rightly said, "Great ideas need landing gear as well as wings". If you can take care of how to say things will move as you would want to.

You are Responsible

Many feel that their superiors at work are responsible for all their ills. First understand that you are alone responsible for your plight. Bosses treat bad workmen with disdain. The same is the case here perhaps. Either take steps to correct and be on course or quit and join elsewhere.

Keep Asking

I keep six honest serving-men
(They taught me all I know);
Their names are What and Why and When
And How and Where and Who.

—Rudyard Kipling

"Ask questions. Even Einstein asked questions" is one nice quotation I came across somewhere.

One way to be sure of what you do is asking people for clarifications. Ask to know about a process, system, a procedure. There is nothing wrong in asking. Being ignorant isn't demeaning but to stay ignorant is. Don't let the fear of being exposed of your ignorance become a road block to your learning efforts. A man becomes learned by asking questions.

"He who is afraid to ask is ashamed of learning" goes a Danish proverb.

Asking people around helps a lot in learning. You will never learn until you have the courage to ask questions. Asking is nothing but a pro-active, self-conscious effort to learn, clarify and develop your knowledge. So keep asking...for more!

Voice Your Problems

A problem well stated is a problem half solved.

—Charles Kettering

Come out with your problems. Keeping them with yourself will not solve them. Moreover, untold are uncared.

Be communicative. 'Speak when you are spoken to' attitude will not help. Again, mono-syllable replies are best avoided. Voice your reservations, issues or problems boldly and get solutions sooner or later, if not, instantly.

Many have a laid back or callous attitude to voice their problems. The reason being they fear or predict they will not be lent a patient hearing. Keep voicing regardless of what the outcome will be. After all, there is nothing wrong in taking efforts than none.

Align Yourself

Aligning yourself in line with the organisation's goals and your boss's plans is most essential. Don't get defensive and turn the tables when someone points your attitude problem by saying, "I don't have an attitude problem. You have a perception problem". Well, you may have your own grudges, grievances against things yet ensure that you don't go out of focus. Your words and deeds directly reflect your attitude towards your work, people and the organisation you work for. Having the right attitude is critical to align yourself with your organisation. If your attitude is not right nothing else is right. And most pathetically, you lose even before you start!

Go Mobile!

Be flexible enough to travel as and when it is required for business purpose. People are reluctant to travel at all and prefer sedentary work style. They quote all 'valid' reasons to avoid relocation and they take refuge in facts, "My kids are too small", "My parents are too old and I have to look after them". It is ironic that the same people who refuse to travel for hardly a week or so would be the first to jump at the chance to go abroad for a month or even more.

Rise to the occasion and avail yourself every opportunity to travel. Travel widens your horizons. Go mobile. You will go places!

Seeing is Believing

Be the first to arrive at office, do your job efficiently and leave later than your boss. It's a sure way of getting to the top. When bosses see you slogging all day long they tend to have a favorable impression about you.

Take Good; Leave Bad

We are influenced by the company we keep — the people with whom we spend much of our time. Over a period of time, you imbibe the qualities, imitate the mannerisms, acquire the style of functioning, mentality of the other person. This will be more pronounced if the other person has influence over you. I mean your boss. You tend to get influenced easily by people superior through close association over time.

Observe and choose only the best. Take only the good and leave the bad. The ant will take only the sugar and leave the sand behind. Or else, you become a classic case for 'Like Boss — Like Subordinate' example. As is the king, so are the subjects. If the boss is aggressive you become one. If he is stingy you too become one. So guard yourself from negative influences as positive things don't easily affect us but the negatives make an impact, sooner or later.

Don't Fret

Career disappointments are common these days. Most of us have the feeling of 'the most wicked, the most lucky' about some of our colleagues who just manage by hook or by crook to piggyback on others. It's a classic case of how one person labors hard but other person gets the credit.

Just understand that in the short-term people may get ahead but in the long-run they will not last long. Remember Marilyn Vos Savant's words,

> "The squeaky wheel may get the most oil, but it's also the first to be replaced".

Anticipate Change

Be ready for change. Without change there is no progress. Most people resist change due to which they earn the wrath of their bosses. There is one secret in feeling at home with change: Change with change or else be left behind. Keep your eyes open and ears close to the ground and jump at the chance...to change.

Profit from Advice

People hate to receive advice particularly those which are unsolicited. Goethe says, "To accept good advice is but to increase one's own ability". Indeed, every one receives advice but it is only the wise who profit from it!

Share Your Ideas

Sharing your ideas with the people around you will show you in the right light. It's in the best interests of ourselves we need to share our ideas with one another. Exchange of views in an unbiased manner will go a long way in widening the horizons.

To illustrate read this: If you have a rupee and I have another, and we exchange, we have one rupee each; if you have a better idea and I have another, and we exchange, we have two better ideas each. It's adding 100% stock in short time. By sharing everyone wins!

Rapport with Boss

If you think your boss is stupid, remember: you wouldn't have a job if he was any smarter.

—John Gotti

Get your equation with your boss right. Your career will be shaped to a great extent by the way your boss views you. Give due respect and extend all courtesies to your boss however 'undeserving' he may be in your opinion. Remember, after all, he is your boss. So keep your boss in good humor. Make sure to portray yourself in the best picture by measuring up to his expectations.

As subordinate you have great responsibility in finishing the tasks to the satisfaction of your superior. Give more than what you get and always measure upto the expectations, better still, exceed them. Never let down him for reasons whatsoever. People who stand by their bosses get rewarded over time. Follow this and you will be the ideal subordinate!

Nothing Comes Free

There is no such thing as free lunch.

—American saying

There is only way to the top. That is by working, pretty hard and taking efforts on our part. The times are very volatile now that people want to get ahead even before they learn to walk. They expect the world to be at their feet at their bidding. Are we doing our duty to make it happen? Do your duty and everything will follow.

No Shortcuts

There are no shortcuts to success.

Work your way up diligently. That's the hallmark of a true worker. None came to a naught by hard work. Nor hard work killed anybody. In all labor there is profit. But don't let profit be your motive. Concentrate on the service you can render.

There is one small secret to disclose. If you measure up to the expectations of your boss, your boss measures upto your expectations. What you give you get. It is as simple as that.

Be Willing to Pay the Price

There are no victories at bargain prices.

—Dwight D. Eisenhower

Almost everything in life comes for a price. If you are prepared to pay the price you get it. If you want something you must be prepared to sacrifice something in return. Great things can be achieved only by great sacrifices. Self-effort is the first step towards achieving what you aspire for. You need to set aside your time, energy and resources for getting what you want. For instance, if you want a promotion, be ready to work for it. The fact that you are merely ready for promotion isn't enough. Are you deserving? That's the moot question.

Successful people find out what it costs to make their dream come true and then make it happen by working towards it.

You Get What You Deserve

You don't get something for nothing.

Don't crib and crave for things to come your way. Get up and work and you will find things you want coming to you. Seek till you find, and you will not lose your labor. There is a lot of link between efforts and results. The law of cause and effect is in full play. Do more you get more. The more you give, the more you receive. It's as simple as no pain, no gain. What goes around comes around.

Work Hard

I find that the harder I work, the more luck
I seem to have.

—Thomas Jefferson

Whoever said, "Better to wear out than to rust out" believed in the value of working hard rather than idling away one's time. Simply, there's no substitute for hard work. Benjamin Franklin said,

> "Waste neither time nor money, but make the best use of both. Without industry and frugality nothing will do and with them everything".

You gain a lot by working for something. You get to appreciate the value of dignity of labor and develop a healthy respect for people who work hard.

You never know what you can do till you try. Diligence makes an expert workman. And these are the people who get rewarded amply. Work hard. Hard work, eventually, pays!

Change Your Attitude

For the diligent the week has seven todays, for the
slothful seven tomorrows.

—Anon

To achieve anything you must have the right attitude, one which is positive. You need an adjustment of attitude to see reason and logic to understand nothing comes without self-exertion. Be prepared to slog it out. You cannot get to the top overnight. As the saying goes, "He who would climb the ladder must begin at the bottom. One step at a time".

There is one crucial difference between people who are self-made millionaires and people who are millionaires by inheritance. Self-made millionaires are proud about themselves, their abilities, their achievements and even if they lose they have the guts to try again and accomplish. The same cannot be necessarily told about millionaires by inheritance.

So work shirkers and idlers, be on your guard. Don't live in a fool's paradise. The world is for those who work. The writing is clear on the wall: "With what measure you give, the same measure you get".

Understand that every moment of laziness is shortening your life span by five minutes. Give up the habit of making excuses. Give results. After all, life is worth living only when you live to the fullest.

Wake up from the slumber, get your act together and get going towards realizing your aspirations. Let your activities help transforming your dreams come true. And finally remember that nothing comes without effort and nothing comes free!

Thriving in Change

Nothing endures but change.

—Heraclites

Today's workplace environments are no longer static like before. They are dynamic and vibrant. Change is the name of the game and change's reach is far and wide. It permeates everywhere. Coping with change and getting the most out of it has become a strategic imperative to keep ourselves in sync and relevant to the work environment.

The very basics of our survival or not in the corporate environment depend on how we perceive and respond to change.

Change Your Mindset

If you don't like something, change it. If you can't change it, change your attitude. Don't complain.

—Maya Angelou

The first step towards accepting change is to change your mindset. Never say no before you have seen or understood. Demolish the mental blockades and be receptive to new ideas. The major problem we face is we are reluctant to let go the old. We are accustomed to things doing it the same way as before and we don't want to change for the good. Change your perception and everything will fall in place.

When to Change?

To change and to change for the better are two different things.

—German proverb

It is true that progress comes by change. But not all change is progress. Just knowing this truth will help in identifying change that is beneficial and those which aren't. Check out what's in store for you, what's good if you accept change and change for the better.

When does Change Happen?

The process of change happens from defying convention, deviating from set precedents, departing from the routine, breaking free from the pattern/stereotype, daring to dream and looking beyond the obvious.

Human endeavor revolve around these basic premises: improvement, betterment than before, development and progress. Out of the inadequacy of the present or when there is a necessity for something better change process starts. Change when it offers something better, is the process which brings progress.

And when it comes to progress, it is said that there are three kinds of people:

1. Those who anticipate change and are prepared to make most of it.
2. Those who react to change and struggle not to be left behind.

3. Those who ignore the change will wonder what happened and will cease to exist.

Digress. You will make progress.

Approaches to Change

It is clear that clinging to the past will make you redundant. The ideal way ahead is to change yourself willingly. There are two approaches to change:

1. Change with the change
2. Change before the change

Change with the Change

He that will not apply new remedies must expect new evils: for time is the greatest innovator.

—Francis Bacon

Most people resist change due to negative attitudes. They are stubborn and obdurate. They are afraid to change the status quo and they feel insecure to adapt themselves to the new environment. They get uncomfortable with the new environment. The single major reason for resistance to change is ignorance. Fear of the unknown and attachment to the present fuels resistance.

People don't bother about change as long as the change doesn't affect them. What they resent is being changed — in adopting new practices and adapting to the new environment.

Ignoring change will stunt your movement further and you will be left behind, sooner or later. Change doesn't threaten you; it's the resistance to change that makes you feel threatened.

If you don't want to be out of sync with the present, the key is in reinventing yourself keeping pace with the changes taking place around you. It is in this willingness and ability to adapt and change yourself lies the challenge. And if you are able to meet that challenge, you make yourself more relevant with the times.

Change is more easier when you figure what's in store for you. Look out for that.

Ideally, become aware of the benefits of the proposed change, acquaint yourself with the finer details and go with the flow. See reason and you will feel there is no point in swimming against the current.

Change before the Change

Change before you have to.

—Jack Welch

If changing with the change is the right thing to do then changing before the change would be the smart thing to do. This smart approach towards change helps you to be future-ready so that when the actual time for change comes you are cool and at home.

Never get lulled by the smooth sailing for the storm is hovering ahead around the corner. Don't get complacent but be alert by scanning the horizon for new opportunities to get better. When you change before the change you are miles ahead of others.

The easiest time to begin a change in direction is when things are going well. The best time to turn around a boat is at the first sight of danger, not after getting caught in a whirlpool. It's your choice to do the right thing or stay smart.

Change Isn't Done Overnight

Transition precedes change. Imposed change will be counter-productive and destructive at times. Abrupt changes aren't welcome. A lot of spadework must be done before bringing about a change. Ushering in change must be preceded by transition. The transition process or phase acquaints people with the new scenario — systems & processes, new people & team, new place, new policy & guidelines, in effect it prepares the ground well for people to warm up.

Transition period enables people to clarify their concerns and apprehensions. It gives the time for looking at things and mentally prepare oneself before accepting change. They don't get caught unawares. Transition is the effective management of surprise which make most people to get thrown off the tracks.

People Change

It is harder to change human nature than to change rivers and mountains.

—English proverb

The process of change starts with individuals. Grandiose plans for change in technology or practices, processes and procedures don't fructify unless people change. You can change anything but people. Preparing them for change is as vital as bringing change. When the microcosm is taken care of macrocosm takes care of itself.

However, don't go gung-ho on whatever that comes as change. Be choosy. Know what's in store for you or the company you work for — today and for tomorrow. After all, what's the fun in going for change when there's nothing to gain by? Change must be for the good of all and must be done in the best interests of the organisation and the elements that make it work — the people.

But remember finally that despite all the change going around you never forget your roots — your core values that make up an individual.

Brace yourself for change. Change is now endemic and it is inevitable. Sail with the wind or better still, change before you have to. After all, change keeps you fit and relevant to the new environment. So gear up for the change and make most of it. That's the ideal way to behave oneself in not just surviving but thriving in change!

Four Follies to Avoid

There are four follies every executive must avoid in order to escape slipping into an abyss called mediocrity:

1. Gossip
2. Lethargy
3. Personal use of business facilities
4. Blame Game

Gossip

Who chatters to you, will chatter of you

Gossip can be juicy and reveal interesting tidbits about the 'gossiped' about person. Such talk has to be avoided at all costs. For, they are fraught with danger. They can be potentially inflammable and can even cause a furore. Slanderous talk, eavesdropping on conversation and exchanging gossip with your colleagues, no matter how well you know them, is better avoided. You never know in which pit which snake resides. People may carry tales about someone and when you unwittingly contribute to it you become a party to it. Soon, no wonder, you will be in the eye of the storm. Just mind your own business and enjoy your work.

Gossiping times are the breeding grounds for rumor and hatred. Gossip makes rumor mills work.

Use coffee and lunch breaks to discuss about general topics. This is one way to avoid gossip. Because, talking about work ends up in gossip. Talk less; work more.

Someone said, "The treacherous, unexplored areas of the world are not in the continents or the seas; they are in the minds and hearts of men". It is very much true of gossipers.

Gossip cheapens the one who gossips more than the one gossiped about. If you are given to making fun of someone, be sure it is of yourself.

Can you trust a person who gossips? When you are with him he gossips about others. The moment you go away from the place you are the latest victim of his gossip.

Only those who don't have enough work start gossiping. If your hands are full you would just mind about doing your business rather talking about others.

When gossipers catch the thread of a conversation, they stretch it into a ball of yarn.

Spin doctors, mischief-makers, rumor-mongers, conspirators, spies and double agents abound places where gossiping takes place. The following are their characteristics:

- These people are self-serving individuals who invent tales where there were none, bad-mouth good people, relish bringing down top achievers, take people for a ride, misinterpret, twist facts to their advantage, involve in character assassinations, poison the new recruits, indulge in dirty tricks and power-politics.

- They poke their noses unnecessarily. They just don't mind their own businesses. For them, other peoples' business is their business.
- These people view someone's loss as their gain — real or imaginary whatsoever.
- Gossipers are cowards who cannot face the gossiped about person directly. The easiest way to take on is to back-bite in their absence.
- They are sadists, hell bent on creating trouble never allowing any one to be at peace.
- They cannot accept or digest when two people are friends. They are out to wreak havoc on rupturing the relationship by back-biting one to the other. 'Divide and rule' is their favorite policy.

Simply, gossipers are human personalities at its worst. Shun at all costs such groups who indulge in gossip.

Lethargy

Laziness is nothing more than the habit of resting before you get tired.

—Jules Renard

People get lethargic due to various reasons. Work shirkers, poor leadership, ineffective supervision, low morale, paltry rewards, etc are some of the causes. Whatever be the reason, lethargy kills action, initiatives. Many people slow down because they fear to finish their tasks on time as they get allotted more work. This fear of work being dumped on them makes them to lose initiatives. Further, work shirking mentality leads to lethargy.

If your job profile is light ask for bigger tasks. Or volunteer around to help people with tougher jobs. "Its-not-my-job" attitude should go.

People who mean business shun lethargic people. Bigger and important tasks never come to them. Don't we avoid queuing up in a counter where the clerk is slow? Today's world wants everything fast and quick, here and now. Be fast enough to catch up with the world.

The most debilitating result with lethargy is that it spells doom for career growth.

Never be idle. Keep your hands full in doing something or the other. Wake up from the stupor and get going.

Now I will let out a secret: A fast worker if he makes mistake people will tolerate. But if a lethargic worker does a mistake people will blow it out of proportion and his life will be hell.

Be slow & passive and your career growth will be slow. Be quick & active your career growth will zoom up. It's as simple as that.

Personal use of Business Facilities

Legend has it that late one evening the Greek envoy, Megasthenes, called on Chanakya. The statesman was busy writing something in the light of an oil lamp. The visitor was asked to wait. Job completed, Chanakya put out the lamp. He then took out another one and lit it. Seeing the perplexed look of Megasthenes, he said, "Till now, I was doing official work. The lamp and oil were out of state funds. Now that I am attending to you in my personal capacity, it is only proper that I use items acquired out of my own funds".

This incident tells us that ethics were not out of place even in ancient times. Probity is necessary when you are among people.

Most of us want to use the facilities given by our organisations for performing official work for personal use. The company-provided telephone, car, laptop, e-mail and the list is endless. Never bring anything even as small as a pencil from workplace. If you follow this scrupulously, you gain credibility in the eyes of your superiors, peers and most important of all — subordinates. People will follow your example and none gets a chance to question your integrity.

Another aspect is most people don't give the attention a work deserves. This is simply because there is no personal gain out of it. The attitude is "Whether I put in my best efforts or not that ain't going to make any difference. Best or shoddy I get my paycheck". Read the following story and you will get the point.

An elderly carpenter was ready to retire. He told his employer-contractor of his plans to leave the house building business and live a more leisurely life with his wife enjoying his extended family. He would miss the paycheck, but he needed to retire. They could get by.

The contractor was sorry to see his good worker go and asked if he could build just one more house as a personal favor. The carpenter said yes, but in time it was easy to see that his heart was not in his work. He resorted to shoddy workmanship and used inferior materials. It was an unfortunate way to end his career.

When the carpenter finished his work and the builder came to inspect the house, the contractor handed the front-door key to the carpenter. "This is your house", he said, "my gift to you".

What a shock! What a shame! If he had only known he was building his own house, he would have done it all so differently. Now he had to live in the home he had built none too well.

So it is with us. We build our lives in a distracted way, reacting rather than acting, willing to put up less than the best. At important points we do not give the job our best effort. Then with a shock we look at the situation we have created and find that we are now living in the house we have built. If we had realized, we would have done it differently.

Think of yourself as the carpenter. Think about your house. Each day you hammer a nail, place a board, or erect a wall. Build wisely. It is the only life you will ever build. Even if you live it for only one day more, that day deserves to be lived graciously and with dignity. The plaque on the wall says, "Life is a do-it-yourself project".

Who could say it more clearly? Your life today is the result of your attitudes and choices in the past. Your life tomorrow will be the result of your attitudes and the choices you make today.

—Source Unknown

Blame Game

He who excuses himself, accuses himself.

—Gabriel Meurier

One of the simplest, meanest and easiest ways to escape when things go wrong is to blame others. When the going gets tough, the weak start blaming. Blaming others will not solve the problem nor achieve results. People who blame others are held in low esteem by others. Beware of the person who gives excuses for failing to do his job. The longer the excuse, the less likely is the truth.

Stop pointing an accusing finger at people for all the ills of yours. Before you point your finger bear in mind that three fingers of your hand points towards you. Set your house in order first. The most crippling failure disease is giving excuses.

With whatever available resources you have to do your best. There is no point in telling around that you could have done better if you had this and that but for their absence explains this shoddy performance. There are no 'ifs' and 'buts'.

Today you may get away blaming people. Tomorrow what will happen if you get to be the boss? The entire responsibility will rest solely on your shoulders. Imagine what will be your position if your staff is going to blame you for their failings.

Just understand the old saying,

"One may fool some people for all the time or all the people for sometime but never all the people for all the time".

One day or other work shirkers and blame gamers are bound to be caught.

Take ownership and responsibility for every assigned task. See to that they are finished in a proper fashion in time. If you stumble on the way, get help. Still you are unable to turnaround, be frank in admitting your fault rather than blaming those who came for help. The frankness to admit when things go wrong is rare among people. Doug Larson's famous quip explains that, "To err is human; to admit it, superhuman".

Commitment and devotion must be there in abundance to finish a job. Though you may get away by blaming people and things it is very obvious for people to see your fickleness and hypocrisy.

The problem with most of us is that we get afflicted by mission amnesia. Don't fall by the way side by getting distracted in things untenable with a responsible and duty-conscious subordinate. Remind yourself, every now and then of the reasons why you come to work and what you are expected in its wake.

It takes guts to rise above the herd to be seen and stand out distinctly. Keep yourself free from these four maladies and you are taken seriously at work. People start valuing you regardless of your grade or position. And that's a sure-fire way to get on to the top!